PRESIDENT TRUMP'S PRO-CHRISTIAN ACCOMPLISHMENTS

STEVE CIOCCOLANTI

PRAISE FROM LEADERS

I was blown away by Steve Cioccolanti's new book and have never seen such a wonderfully-crafted, biblically-based prospective on godly leadership. This is so balanced that after reading it for yourself, I'm sure that you would agree with me that God has chosen His leader for the White House. I am equally sure that President Trump would be thoroughly encouraged by reading it for himself.

Kevin Jessip
President of Global Strategic Alliance
Founder and co-chair of TheReturn.org

In 2020 America, God has blessed us with a prayerful, pro-life 45th President for nearly four years. This book, a comprehensive view of President Trump's accomplishments, is evidence that God has not forsaken America.

Alveda Celeste King
Director of Civil Rights for The Unborn
Niece of Civil Rights Leader Dr. Martin Luther King Jr.

As usual, Steve Cioccolanti's insights are Biblically powerful, pragmatic and prophetically eye-opening. A must-read.

Allan Parker
President of The Justice Foundation

President Trump's Pro-Christian Accomplishments

Published by **Discover Media**

P.O. Box 379, Black Rock, VIC 3193, AUSTRALIA

www.Discover.org.au

Publisher's Note: *Scripture verses sometimes end in a dangling punctuation (e.g. comma or quotation mark) instead of a period. These are not errors but are quoted as is.*

The publisher is not responsible for websites or their content that are not owned by the publisher.

Book cover design by: Esther Eunioo Jun & Selena Sok

ISBN paperback: 978-1-922273-24-6

ISBN ebook: 978-1-922273-25-3

Second Printing. Printed in the U.S.A.

DEDICATION

To my father, mother, and
daughter Amber-Radiance.

When my third child was born, I was working on *Trump's Unfinished Business: 10 Prophecies to Save America*. At St. John's Hospital, I juggled the baby and a laptop, giving Amber-Radiance her first baths and rushing back to the laptop whenever I wasn't needed by my wife or our baby. So it was appropriate that I dedicated it to her and her siblings with hopes for their bright future.

By the time I finished this book, *President Trump's Pro-Christian Accomplishments*, Amber-Radiance was reaching for my laptop and smacking my keyboard like an author. She had just turned one year old. She is part of the "lockdown baby" generation, who's not been to a playground or interacted with adults outside her family and without masks. How unprecedented the year 2020 has been. There is nothing normal about it.

Now more than ever, children need a defender of their rights and freedom. They need to know to know that the human longing for liberty and for connection with God and family are normal. It's my prayer that one day she will pick up this book and read about a leader whom she will not remember, but whose presidency will be studied for years to come.

I finished my part in writing *President Trump's Pro-Christian Accomplishments* on my mother's 72nd birthday. She was born the same year as Israel in 1948. I received the education I did through her sacrifice and that of my father Mark Cioccolanti.

So I dedicate this book to my parents and their youngest granddaughter. I love you.

CONTENTS

...I will teach you the good and the right way...
for consider what GREAT things He has done for you.
1 Samuel 12:23-24

★ ★ ★ ✝ ★ ★ ★

INTRODUCTION

Is Donald Trump a Christian? Is he God's choice? How are his actions affecting Christians, Israel and Bible prophecy? As a Bible teacher, I hear these questions all the time.

As I started searching for answers and compiling his pro-Christian actions into a book, I thought it would be a mini-book, perhaps a small pamphlet for a few Christians. I also thought that the list might feel "dated" as soon as the elections of 2020 were over. But I was wrong on both counts.

I learned important lessons I would like to summarize. Here are three timeless takeaways from this list of President Trump's pro-Christian accomplishments:

1. The Lord is a redeeming God.

If Trump is half as bad as the media says he is (they call him deranged, unhinged, a racist, a pathological liar), and our Lord can still work through him to advance the pro-life movement, release Christians out of prisons, pass criminal reform, and negotiate peace in the Middle East and on the Korean peninsula, then God can surely use you no matter what you've done wrong in the past.

EPHESIANS 2:4-5

But God, who is rich in mercy, because of His great love with which He loved us, even when we were dead in trespasses, made us alive together with Christ (by grace you have been saved),

2. The man is working very hard.

Despite being called all sorts of shameful names that would qualify him as the least Christian man on earth, hardly anyone would accuse him of being lazy.[1] Trump is getting more done to advance the Kingdom than many of us who call ourselves Christian and attend church every week.

Trump sleeps four hours a day, speaks with boundless energy, fights terrorists and negotiates tirelessly with hostile politicians. How productive are we by comparison? How many enemies do we have by comparison? What's our excuse for not putting in a little extra effort?

None.

We each have the same amount of time—24 hours a day. As the father of modern advertising David Ogilvy said, "Hard work never killed a man. Men die of boredom...They do not die of hard work."

Start early in the day. Start early in life if you can. Leave this world a better place than when you first entered it. Listen to what the most productive person who ever lived said to His parents at the age of twelve.

LUKE 2:49-50

And He said to them, "Why did you seek Me? Did you not know that I must be about My Father's business?" But they did not understand the statement which He spoke to them.

We live in an age of delayed maturation. I think some

people do think that hard work *will* kill them! If we believe Jesus is coming soon, we'd better waste no time, start early, and work hard.

3. The enemy is more deceptive than most Christians realize. To separate fact from fiction, I had a team of seven capable people in America and Australia research what President Trump had done. It was not easy for us to find anything positive about Trump on the Internet. Anecdotally, we found Google search results heavily biased against him.

This level of monopoly on information is unprecedented in human history. On June 16, 2019, Dr. Robert Epstein, a research psychologist and former editor-in-chief of *Psychology Today*, appeared before the US Senate Judiciary Subcommittee to explain why Google's monopoly on search presents a serious threat to democracy and human freedom. Among his findings, he reported:

"In 2016, biased search results generated by Google's search algorithm likely impacted undecided voters in a way that gave at least 2.6 million votes to Hillary Clinton (whom I supported) ...Google search results...were significantly biased in favor of Secretary Clinton in all 10 positions on the first page of search results...votes shift when search results favor one candidate, cause, or company.

I call this shift "SEME" – the Search Engine Manipulation Effect.... My recent research demonstrates that Google's "autocomplete" search suggestions can turn a 50/50 split among undecided voters into a 90/10 split without people's awareness...Google has likely been determining the outcomes of upwards of 25 percent of the national elections worldwide since at least 2015. This is because many races are very close and because **Google's persuasive technologies are very powerful.**"[2]

This is why throughout the book, I was careful to include as many primary sources and first-hand quotes as possible. In many instances, this will be the first time you will hear President Trump in his own words without the quick TV edits or pundits' spin. "Spin" is a technique the media uses to intentionally mislead people by reporting negative events favorably (like calling violent rioters and looters "peaceful protesters") or reporting positive events unfavorably.

An example of the latter was when President Trump met with six American hostages whom his administration helped to free from foreign imprisonment. How could the established media spin such a positive story?

The New York Times led the positive story with a negative: "With a thin record of achievement abroad, President Trump celebrated the releases of Americans held overseas."[3] Thin record? If you were to mention that Trump had just negotiated peace between Israel and the UAE, defeated the ISIS caliphate, and cancelled unfair deals like TPP,[4] NAFTA,[5] and the Iran deal ("the worst deal ever negotiated" according to the President), the media would retort, "Embattled at Home, Trump Finds Himself Isolated Abroad, Too."[6] It's difficult to please someone who's out to get you. There is no logic in or reasoning with someone hired to stir your emotions. So I could not rely much on secondary sources like the corporate media.

I kept my list fact-based, following this pattern: date, accomplishment, and Scripture (where appropriate). You will see clearly where I interject my commentary, mainly to explain the meaning of Scripture.

• • • † • • •

If you're a speed reader, I highly recommend that you slow down to absorb at least these four speeches by President Trump:

- January 28, 2018 — his most important speech against "globalism" (the concentration of power in the hands of a few), delivered in the den of globalists —Davos.
- January 21, 2020 — his clearest rebuke of global warming / climate change fanatics.
- June 21, 2020 — his most dangerous speech against the Deep State, reminiscent of JFK's speech on the same topic in 1961.
- August 28, 2020 — his most comprehensive 2020 campaign speech at the RNC, delivered at the White House.

These speeches should be studied in full by students, so they can form their own conclusions, rather than being simply told what to think by the media. Of course, all the events in this book have been included because they are significant and complete a holistic picture of Trump's stance towards God, Christianity, Israel and the Bible.

★ ★ ★ ✝ ★ ★ ★

STATEMENT OF PURPOSE

This is not a political book. I spend no time criticizing the "other side." Any juxtaposition is fact-based. As I tweeted on August 13, 2020: "I'd prefer an honest Democrat over a deceptive Republican any day."[1] And vice versa.

The Lord asked me to write this book not to influence an election, but to set the record straight about what He is doing in America...what He would like to do throughout the world. There are not many courageous leaders who will do a thankless job for little gain. President Trump's net wealth has declined from $3.7 billion in 2016[2] to $2.1 billion in 2020.[3] He has taken a pay cut as President to work harder than he did as a private citizen. He has donated every Presidential paycheck he's received. He is literally working for free for the American people.

Yet he is not poor; I believe in God's sight he is rich in pro-Christ, pro-Christian, and pro-church accomplishments. The Apostle Paul lamented the greatest poverty in the world: the paucity of people who truly seek to do the Creator's will.

★ ★ ★ ✝ ★ ★ ★

PHILIPPIANS 2:20-21

For I have no one like-minded, who will sincerely care for your state. For all seek their own, not the things which are of Christ Jesus.

These verses are not speaking of non-believers—they would, of course, seek their own. Why would they seek the things of Christ? These verses tell us that you can be a Christian and not pursue God's will for your life. To be a Christian, you need faith in Christ. To be in God's perfect will, you need good works. Neither can substitute for the other, but together, faith and works make a life that is well-pleasing to God.

CHAPTER 1

IS TRUMP GOD'S CHOICE?

If I am not doing the works of my Father, then do not believe me; but if I do them, even though you do not believe me, believe the works....
John 10:37-38 (ESV)

ONE OF THE doubts Christians had about Donald Trump in 2016 was whether he was playing us, or would he really deliver on his campaign promises. Nominating pro-life justices to the Supreme Court and moving the US Embassy to Jerusalem were promises that other presidential candidates had made to Christian voters, only to backpedal after they were elected to office.

Donald Trump delivered on both counts from 2016 to 2020.

Jesus gave us a very simple principle to objectively get to know someone about whom we are in doubt: if you don't believe him, believe his works; if he does the works, even if you don't believe in him as a person, believe the works. Jesus laid out this rule in Matthew chapter 7.

MATTHEW 7:17-20

> **Even so, every good tree bears good fruit, but a bad tree bears bad fruit. A good tree cannot bear bad fruit, nor can a bad tree bear good fruit. Every tree that does not bear good fruit is cut down and thrown into the fire. Therefore by their fruits you will know them.**

How do we know whether Donald Trump is God's choice?

There are at least two ways. The first is by preternatural confirmations or prophetic signs—fortuitous circumstances that are clearly beyond a person's own power or pre-planning. This will be the subject of another book. The second is by the works, not the personality, style or oration skill. Does the man keep his campaign promises?

We've come to expect politicians to routinely break promises. "No new taxes" before election becomes raised taxes during the administration.[1] "You can keep your plan...you can keep your doctor" before Obamacare becomes "you can't keep either" after the legislation has passed.

PolitiFact called Obama's promise "the lie of the year in 2013."[2] Under Obamacare millions of Americans lost their prior plans and many lost access to their doctors. Far from covering every American, Obamacare left 28 million Americans uninsured after 10 years.[3]

Premiums did not go down by $2,500 for the average family, as Obama promised—they went up nearly $3,000! According to the Department of Health and Human Services (HHS), "Average individual market premiums more than doubled from $2,784 per year in 2013 to $5,712 on Healthcare.gov in 2017—an increase of $2,928 or 105%."[4]

Yet Obama is loved by the media and Trump is hated. The justification is not one of substance but of style. The argument from mainstream media boils down to feelings: Obama has a likable personality and charisma, whereas Trump is, in their opinion, mean, unhinged, and lacking compassion.

JOHN 7:24

Do not judge according to appearance, but judge with righteous judgment.

Jesus tells us to judge a leader by his works, not his words, his style and certainly not his appearance. The Pharisees judged John the Baptist on his appearance, alleging "he has a demon," probably because he wore camel's hair, ate locusts, and preached in the dirty desert.[5] Yet no one was more demon-possessed than those who murdered the Son of God. Today the same people who claim Trump lacks compassion also advocate for the murder of babies and condone street violence against Americans who don't share their political slant. The position is so absurd it's an affront to any sense of morality.

The media talks derisively about Donald Trump's skin color and hair. Imagine them doing that with a black person or a woman.

You can't.

Double standards are a sign of deceptive people: one rule for you, another for me (and my team). Christians should rise above that. We should be consistent and follow the Lord's policy. What does the record show about Donald Trump's first term? What did he promise to do? Did he keep his promises?

APPOINT THE RIGHT JUDGES

Actually, he over-delivered on his main promises that got him elected in 2016. He appointed not only two pro-life justices to the US Supreme Court—Justices Neil Gorsuch and Brett Kavanaugh—but over the past three years, the Senate has confirmed 203 of President Trump's judicial nominees.[6]

Out of the 203, Trump has appointed 53 circuit court judges[7], 146 District Court judges, as well as two judges for the

Court of International Trade.[8] These appointments are not perfunctory.

DEFEND RELIGIOUS FREEDOM

Wayne Grudem of TownHall remarked:

"Trump's two Supreme Court appointments have already been responsible for highly significant cases that increase religious freedom, such as the decisions

(1) to allow state aid that is given to non-religious schools to be given also to religious schools (Montana decision);

(2) to protect the right of religious schools to hire and fire employees based on the school's religious convictions; and

(3) to allow religious groups to be exempt from government regulations that would otherwise cause them to violate their consciences in matters of birth control..."[9]

The Washington Post lamented in December 2019, "1 in every 4 circuit court judges is now a Trump appointee. After three years in office, President Trump has remade the federal judiciary, ensuring a conservative tilt for decades and cementing his legacy no matter the outcome of November's election."[10] Let me translate what a "conservative tilt" means: pro-life.

SAVE THE CHILDREN

The one issue that the radical left cares most about is sex—sex with anyone, anytime, without any consequences. This is the defining issue of the left. In Australia, there is at least one honest left-leaning party: the "Sex Party." Citizens are offended by the truth, so the party which formed in 2017 learned to mask their agenda by rebranding themselves in 2018 as the "Reason Party."

The sex-driven agenda of the radical left has led to the

mistreatment of children on many levels: abortion, pedophilia and early sexualization in public school education. One Californian senator is now calling for the decriminalization of gay sex with minors, because criminalizing pedophilia would be discrimination against the LGBTQ community.[11]

The issue of aborting babies and abusing children is central to the left's agenda. It is not hidden. They want it to go mainstream. In August 2020, Netflix promoted a French film called *Cuties*, featuring scantily clad 11-year-old girls twerking and doing other hyper-sexualized moves. The left did not condemn this. No, they gave *Cuties* an award at the Sundance Festival in 2017.[12]

With cultural and political forces pushing for normalization of sex with anyone, at any age, without any consequence, you can see why so many celebrities hate Trump. He and a bunch of his conservative judges are standing in their way to a sexual revolution. Sex is not a side issue for the left—it is their non-negotiable core issue.

Trump proclaimed January 22, 2020, a "Day of National Sanctity of Human Life." On January 24, Donald Trump became the first US President in history to attend the March for Life in Washington, DC. At this important pro-life event he said, "We're here for a very simple reason: to defend the right of every child, born and unborn, to fulfill their God-given potential."[13]

PROTECT THE ONLY DEMOCRACY IN THE MIDDLE EAST

Trump surpassed the most optimistic expectations concerning Israel. On December 6, 2017 he made America the first country to recognize Jerusalem as the "Eternal Capital" of Israel. "Today, we finally acknowledge the obvious: that Jerusalem is Israel's capital. This is nothing more, or less, than a recognition of reality. It is also the right thing to do. It's something that has to be done," Trump said from the White House's Diplomatic Reception Room.

The US Embassy officially relocated from Tel Aviv to Jerusalem on May 14, 2018, to coincide with the 70th anniversary of Israel's Declaration of Independence.

Trump further recognized Israel's sovereignty over the Golan Heights by proclamation on March 25, 2019. To top it off, he supported Israel's right to annex Biblical Samaria, or the area known today as the West Bank or Jordan Valley. Samaria is not only historic Israel where Abraham, Isaac and Jacob encountered God, it is also a strategic buffer zone of defense and a gateway to the country's natural lifeline—the Jordan River.

Trump's critics condemned him and his pro-Israeli acts. They claimed his support of Israel would incense the Palestinians. They claimed Trump would start a war in the Middle East.

Did he?

On August 13, 2020, the United Arab Emirates (UAE) became the first Arab nation in 26 years to declare a peace agreement with Israel. Trump's tough negotiation was exactly what the Middle East was not used to from American presidents, but respected. I did not say they liked it. They preferred career politicians who kicked the proverbial can down the street so the next politician can kick it again.

Within a few days of this peace agreement, Lebanese President Michel Aoun expressed his willingness to establish normal relations with Israel.[14] The timing was ripe. It was one of those divine moments when you know the right man for the right job had come at the right time. After the mushroom cloud explosion at the port of Beirut on August 4, which killed 171 and injured 6,000 people,[15] the Lebanese had had enough of Hezbollah.

Although the cause of the explosion is still under investigation, the survivors on the ground suspected that the Hezbollah-controlled port served as storage for the explosive ingredient ammonium nitrate that Hezbollah bought in large quantities in 2013 and 2014. The Beirut port was being used as a smuggling hub for weapons and explosives by the Shi'ite groups Hezbollah and the Iranian Quds Force. The Lebanese people have decided that they are fed up with their terrorist political party, their worthless currency and their crashed economy.

Suddenly the prospect of peace in the Middle East looks more attractive than destroying Israel. It also appears saner and more possible in the age of Trump.

For decades, no politician had been able to solve the problem of the Middle East. Ceasefires were declared and violated. Peace deals were signed and broken. Diplomacy faltered. No one in power was serious about cleaning up the mess in the Middle East.

Yes, they talked of cleaning up...and talked...and talked. But President Trump made the Middle East his priority, visiting Saudi Arabia and Israel in his first foreign trip in May 2017. I was in Israel at the same time, leading a Biblical tour. Trump arrived with a big broom and swept away the lackadaisical status quo.

Trump's style does not make sense to career politicians because he acts with a businessman's acumen. The world wondered: How can a businessman solve a problem politicians could not since 1948? By making the United States the world's largest oil producer—effectively energy independent for the first time in history—Trump took away the "oil card" from the Arabs. He removed it off the negotiating table.

Arab leaders saw the writing on the wall. They could no longer pull geopolitical strings by merely being exporters of oil. Though global oil prices will still be affected by global markets,

(1) America did not need their export anymore, (2) their oil would run out eventually, and (3) new energy sources were being developed worldwide. It was a trifecta of changes that the Middle East could no longer ignore.

The proposition President Trump made to the Middle East was the same one he made to Kim Jong Un in June 2018 and June 2019: you could be a lot richer if you stopped fighting your neighbor and joined the rest of the world in peaceful coexistence. The Middle East took this offer seriously. They have been missing out on commerce, technology, tourism, and other benefits of peace and freedom.

THE FALSE PEACE

Some Christians with an eschatological view that the anti-Christ must appear in the Middle East and a war must be staged at Armageddon (*Har Megiddo* in Israel) are suspicious of any peace in the Middle East. A peace deal by a politician might suggest he's the anti-Christ. They argue, correctly I would add, that any peace on earth is temporary, and the only true peace will come from the Prince of Peace.

But the Prince of Peace also said, "Blessed are the peacemakers, for they shall be called sons of God" (Matthew 5:9 ESV). A politician trying to make peace on earth is not the anti-Christ; he's called a son of God!

King David wrote, "Take note of the one who has integrity! Observe the godly! For the one who promotes peace has a future" (Psalm 37:37 NET).

The Holy Spirit instructs Christians to pray for our leaders, "that we may lead a quiet and PEACEABLE life in all godliness and honesty. For this is good and acceptable in the sight of God our Saviour; Who will have all men to be saved, and to come unto the knowledge of the truth" (1 Timothy 2:2-4 KJV).

Yes, there will come a false peacemaker who will betray

Israel in the end times. This betrayer will indeed be the anti-Christ, which is another name for the ultimate anti-Semite.

Christians should not live in anticipation of one bad leader, but in continual service to our Lord. Christians should not live in expectation of one war predicted in the Bible. We should work toward peace. "If it is possible, as much as depends on you, live peaceably with all men" (Romans 12:18).

We pursue peace, because peace is a platform for preaching of the Gospel. People ravaged by war have neither time nor freedom to go to church and hear many sermons. They are living in fear, fleeing mortal danger, or subsisting in survival mode. Such people are not generally open to spiritual enlightenment. The most open-minded ones during war are often oppressed and imprisoned. People living in peace are much more likely to be open to hearing the Gospel.

In this sense, Trump's undiplomatic negotiation style—his "Art of the Deal"—has done more to open up the Middle East to peace, and eventually to the Gospel, than any politician has ever done. Some politicians are all stick and no carrot; other politicians are all carrot and no stick. Trump brought both the stick (justice) and the carrot (peace).

Trump ended ISIS' reign of terror in the region. He aggressively pursued known terrorist leaders. He ordered strikes that eliminated three terrorist masterminds:

(1) the leader of ISIS Abu Bakr al-Baghdadi, killed in October 2019;

(2) the world's #1 terrorist General Qasem Soleimani, killed in January 2020; and

(3) the founder of al-Qaeda in Yemen Qasim al-Rimi, killed in February 2020.

Trump negotiated the peace agreement between Israel and the UAE. The Middle East seems ready not only to normalize relations with its long-standing enemy Israel, but I predict, it will also embrace tolerance by welcoming other religions to worship in the region. When this happens, it will be a historic and prophetic breakthrough that moves us much closer to Jesus' Second Coming.

ORANGE MAN BAD[16]

Yet Christians remain skeptical about Trump. Prominent pastor and author Max Lucado did not believe Trump had the character to be a Christian or a leader; he wrote a scathing review of Trump that was published by *The Washington Post* on February 26, 2016.[17] (My comments on Christian criticism of Trump is in the next chapter if you're interested.)

The media beats the drum every day that the sky will fall, the world will end, and democracy will disappear if Donald Trump tweets as President.

Is this narrative believable? Back in 2016, the media predicted that the world would end and the economy would crash with Donald Trump's election. They also predicted that North Korea would have a nuclear war with America. They predicted Trump would start a nuclear war with Iran.

If you listened to the media alone, you'd believe that war and human extinction were inevitable; his unpredictable behavior and his undiplomatic personality would surely lead us into war.

But the opposite happened.

For the first time in over 40 years, a US administration has not started a new war. Young Americans have not been sent to die in more countries they cannot locate on a map before going. A peace prize should be created for Donald Trump in recognition of this achievement.

Surely corporate media could not spin it...but they did. They said, "Trump 'isolated' America."[18] They complained, "Trump is weak on dictators...in fact, Trump is weak on dictators because Trump is a dictator."[19]

THE REAL DICTATORS

Those who believe Trump is Hitler fail to understand three things.

First, America has three branches of government and none can take complete control of the nation. This is called the "separation of powers." Every American student would have learned this in American history class.

Second, the Executive branch has a two-term limit guaranteed by the Twenty-Second Amendment, which Congress approved in 1947 and the states ratified by 1951. Trump cannot be a dictator because after two terms, he will have to vacate the office of the President.

A dictator is someone who can stay in power for life, like Recep Erdogan of Turkey and Xi Jingping of China can. But the media elites don't seem to hate all dictators to the same degree as they hate Donald Trump.

Third, Trump has had many opportunities to consolidate executive power during the crises of 2020, notably the coronavirus pandemic and the riots that spread from Minneapolis to Seattle. Instead, the President let Governors decide their own states' COVID19 policies. He also let mayors ruin their own cities (as they did in Chicago and Seattle), or protect them with police, law and order. Unfortunately for the conspiracy theorists, it turned out Donald Trump was not a dictator.

In other Western countries like Australia and New Zealand, prime ministers and premiers seized every opportunity to consolidate their power and pass new laws to give themselves more power[20]. They did not mind eroding the people's fundamental rights and freedom. Curfews and heavy fines for minor infractions were imposed. Constant state surveillance of private citizens using drones, mobile apps and "contact tracing" is being proposed. Yet few journalists called these power grabbers a Hitler or a dictator.

Christians, don't ever be blinded by a party spirit! No Christian should subscribe to all the views of any political party. No Christian should belong to the "lifelong" category of party affiliation which can become a modern form of idolatry. Our allegiance should be to the Truth.

Our doubts about Donald Trump should be confirmed or denied by his actions. The trouble is that it is so hard to find objective news and facts about his actions on the Internet.

IS TRUMP GOD'S CHOICE?

The main purpose of this book is to list Trump's most pro-Christ, pro-Christian, and pro-church achievements for the past four years. Christians should judge him by his works as President, not by emotionally-charged soundbites from the controlled media.

The second purpose of this book is to encourage you to discover God's calling for your own life, because God's calling matters.

I'm good at what I do, not because I'm good, but because God *called* me. He called me to write books for Him. He called me to make videos on YouTube, Vimeo and my online church community app.[21] I am not smart enough, funny enough, or well-connected enough to have 45 million views on YouTube on my own. The calling makes a difference. When you do what you're called to do, God's grace vastly improves your own strength and mental capacity. There is a supply of the Holy Spirit because God wants the job done and you know He will get the credit!

No one is qualified to be President. Nothing can train you. No amount of information can save you from your flaws. Donald Trump seems to be able to handle the pressures that would crush an ordinary person because God *called* him. In fact, he seems to thrive in his calling to negotiate tough deals with powerful people.

The question Christians should ask during each election is not, "Who do I like?" It's "Who did God *call* to do His will for the next 4 years?"

How can you know whether God called someone? You know someone's calling by their works. You can ignore the media. You can ignore the war of words and emotions. Look for the God-factor! Look for the works!

I will be the first person to tell you Trump is not right about everything. I do not subscribe to party lines. I have criticized conservatives for preaching limited government but expanding government spending and departments as much as liberals. When President Trump approved the creation of a new military branch called the "Space Force," I suggested in my book *Trump's Unfinished Business* that a better alternative would be to keep that role where it naturally belongs—in the Navy.[22]

In chapter 5 about *Draining the Financial Swamp,* I wrote the following:

"...the Navy already has assets that can fight in space—modified AEGIS destroyers and cruisers. As of 2017, it has 22 ships equipped with anti-space-missiles and capable of shooting down spy satellites.

"...Sci-Fi writers realize that space exploration is analogous to ocean exploration, and the space crew are analogous to navy crew. That is why they use Navy ranks almost invariably for the crew of starships.

"Use the Navy."

The President did not take my suggestion. I believe Donald Trump is repeating the same mistake Ronald Reagan made when he launched the Strategic Defense Initiative (dubbed "Star Wars") in 1983. Ten years later it was a dud and had to be discontinued. Government bureaucracies are money-sucking monsters. We don't need new ones when we can improve existing ones.

People make mistakes. Every believer in the Bible did, but they are still believers. Aren't you glad? The President should be able to make some mistakes—sincere ones—without being called a liar.

Before examining the track record of Donald Trump from a Christian point of view, we should address a serious Christian objector.

CHAPTER 2

CHRISTIAN CRITICISM OF CANDIDATE TRUMP

WITH 130 MILLION books in print and named "America's pastor" in 2005 by *Christianity Today*, Max Lucado is on nearly every Christian bookshelf. His views are influential and his 2016 blog against Donald Trump would qualify him as Trump's most high-profile Christian critic. If you are not interested in Max Lucado's views, you can skip this chapter.

I would like to emphasize that I do not usually name ministers in a negative light (we ought to lift and build up one another) and I don't intend to here. I also would like to make clear that Lucado stated his views before President Trump achieved all that he has done, and perhaps he has amended his views.[1] But after four years, his blog remains on his website with no retraction, so I must proceed on the basis that his blog remains a current Christian argument against Trump.

None of us have the time to investigate every single claim we hear—we have our own lives to live—so we rely on authoritative figures to tell us what's most important. For many people, they accept the views presented to them by the media. I saw how fast people parroted the media without question during the coronavirus outbreak. For Christians, we may adopt the views of our favorite authors, like C.S. Lewis, even though

C.S. Lewis may not be correct about the subject of the Holy Spirit and His present-day work, for instance.

Lucado is a superb thinker and writer, an authority in Christendom; therefore, many Christians would adopt his views without spending too much time to compare them to Scriptures. This is what we want to do here.

On February 24, 2016, the prominent pastor and author blogged that he did not believe Trump had the character worthy to be a President, much less a Christian President. His scathing review of Trump was published by the *Washington Post* on February 26, 2016.[2]

As a fellow pastor and author, I fully empathize with Lucado's desire for a well-spoken President. He compared electing a President to interviewing a boy wishing to date his daughter—the candidate should at least be "decent." He lamented Trump's "insensitivities" and hoped for "a return to verbal decency."

The qualities Lucado was looking for come precisely from his experience as a pastor. We pastors change lives with words. Sermons are our craft. Words are the tools of our trade.

But this precisely is also why we may be myopic when it comes to God's qualifications for a leader. A typical soft-spoken pastor would be ill-suited for the Presidency. Which Christian leader do you personally know who could have negotiated with Kim Jong Un and wiped out ISIS?

I know a lot of pastors and I know of none who could have brought peace and justice to the Middle East like Trump has. Few pastors could have lasted under the intense scrutiny and pressure Trump has faced. I have witnessed too many ministers quit their callings over far less negative press than Trump has received. What if God is not calling a talker to the White House, but an avenger like Cyrus and Nebuchadnezzar?

I have traveled to over 40 countries carrying the Gospel to some of the most remote places. The "dirtiest" room I've ever entered was not a house of idols in Asia or Africa, but a political meeting in the State of Victoria.

I could feel the hate in the air.

Not long after that experience, Victoria was put under what most people believe to be the worst coronavirus lockdown in the world. It did not surprise me. It was my observation that these political players were nasty to each other and had little regard for family values, human rights or religious freedom.

Politics is toxic.

The public is hardly aware of the antics and tactics insiders use to backstab good people, leak their information to the media and get rid of Christian candidates. It has been my experience that some conservatives and liberals have tried to minimize any Christian influence in public life.

I am certain that the type of soft-spoken speaker Lucado wished for would fail to do half the job President Trump has done. It's my job to watch orators, and I have seen many politicians dazzle the public with their stream of words.

In Australia, there is currently a soft-spoken Prime Minister who claims to be Christian. I have prayed for him and had high hopes he would genuinely live out his Christian faith in public service. He courted the Christians and won their votes.

However, Jesus told us to judge a man not by his speeches, but by his results. It would appear, if all accounts are true, that Prime Minister Scott Morrison did not defend the Pakistani Christian Asia Bibi when she was sentenced to death by hanging for blasphemy. Australia was supposed to be a beacon of religious freedom and human rights in the region. Australia was the most natural place to welcome her as a refugee; instead Americans rescued her out of Pakistan and she settled in Canada in May 2019.

PM Morrison did not defend Israel Folau, a rugby player who was persecuted for posting his Christian views on social media, to the extent that one might expect him to. Folau lost his

$3 million contract and other sponsorships. In a stunning admission about the dismissal, the CEO of Rugby Australia, Raelene Castle, admitted that the Bible itself was the problem for her. She said she would have fired Folau if he had "photocopied Bible passages" and posted them to his social media.[3]

This would have been the time for a Christian national leader to stand up in defense of free speech, but Mr. Morrison left him to hang. It is a shame that Folau, the record holder for most tries scored in Super Rugby history, is now employed by a French rugby team, the Catalans Dragons.

It took a lot of courage for Folau to continue speaking about his faith during the Australian Bushfires of 2019-2020, suggesting it may be a "judgment of God." While I personally disagree that the bush fires had to do with the legalization of same-sex marriage in Australia (85% of bush fires were caused by human agents accidentally starting one or committing arson[4]), I still believe in Folau's right to free speech. The Bible does say that God judges nations for sins and He saves nations for repenting. This is a balanced view. But instead the Prime Minister lambasted Folau for his "appallingly insensitive comments."[5]

Based upon these examples, it seems that if you're a Christian in Australia or abroad, Mr. Morrison will not defend you even if secularists attack your faith. PM Morrison is too nice, too sensitive, and too genteel. He reaches out to the opposing side, so much so that one cannot tell that there are two sides on the political spectrum about family values, religious liberties or "health dictatorships"—a term his predecessor Tony Abbott used to describe the State of Victoria run by the Labor Party.[6]

Constitutional law professor Augusto Zimmermann wrote, "Scott Morrison has publicly backed the Victorian Premier, including his imposing of de facto martial law across the State.

'Daniel Andrews has my full support. I will give him every support he needs,' says the Prime Minister."[7]

The lockdown in Victoria is possibly the harshest in the world and includes business shutdown, stay at home curfews by 8:00 p.m., closed borders, prohibition of interstate and international travel, and harsh penalties for minor infractions. On August 3, 2020, a pregnant woman was arrested and handcuffed in her own home for posting on her Facebook about a Freedom March to protest the lockdown.[8] She posted that protesters should obey the law by wearing face masks and maintaining social distancing, warning everyone that she did not want anyone to get arrested. By contrast, the police arrested no one in connection to the tens of thousands who marched for Black Lives Matter just a few months earlier when the coronavirus lockdown was in effect.

Why should Americans care what's happening in Australia? Because the effect of silver-tongued politicians on our freedom is not conjecture—it's not theory—it's a reality. If Max Lucado would like a sensitive-sounding man to be President, then Christians would get a Scott Morrison or Daniel Andrews instead of a Donald Trump.

Because Max Lucado is one of the most well-respected Christian leaders, I believe he will have a high regard for God's Word on this matter. It's not personal opinion that matters to us. It's not personality preferences that matter to God. We need the harmony of Scriptures to form the right doctrine on leadership.

My first Biblical question is, "Would King David pass Max Lucado's decency test?"

David said about a business owner named Nabal, the man who denied him and his men food and water, **"Let God do so and more also unto the enemies of David if I leave of all that pertain to him by the morning light any that piss against the wall" (1 Samuel 25:22 JUB).**

Was David's language really necessary? Could David have chosen his words more wisely? Why the extreme reaction to a foolish man from a man of God? Why not choose the "higher road" and ignore Nabal?

Instead, David said he would not only kill Nabal, but all who "piss against the wall."

My second Biblical question is, "Would Max Lucado invite David to speak in his church after hearing this?"

I think he would. Because God himself called David a man after God's own heart. It simply doesn't get better than that for a guest speaker!

My third Biblical question is, "Would Max Lucado elect David to be President if he had the chance?"

Without a doubt. How could any pastor disqualify a man whom God Himself said will be "king forever"?[9] Yet this royal ancestor of the Messiah had a temper and an unfiltered mouth.

One reason King David and Donald Trump are alike is that both of them have a strong sense of loyalty and expectation of reciprocity. I've found through my 20 years of pastoring that sweet talkers are not more loyal or more honorable than rough talkers. David could not stand Nabal because he was dishonorable—he did not reciprocate a good deed.

Likewise, Trump cannot stand politicians like Mitt Romney. Trump endorsed Romney in the 2012 Presidential election and again in the 2018 US Senate race, despite Romney being his worst GOP critic. Romney became the only Republican who voted to convict Trump in the 2020 impeachment trial. Romney now has the dubious honor of being the first US Senator in history to vote to remove a President from his own party. Would Lucado consider the soft-spoken Romney principled or vengeful? Would Romney be better qualified to be President?

Based on the Biblical record of leaders, God does not call only soft-spoken, mild-mannered people to do His will. When God called on Isaiah to be a prophet, Isaiah's immediate response was, "Woe is me, for I am undone! Because I am a man of **unclean lips**, And I dwell in the midst of a people of **unclean lips**; For my eyes have seen the King, The LORD of hosts" (Isaiah 6:5).

The New Living Translation says Isaiah had "filthy lips." The New English Translation says his "lips are contaminated by sin." In modern language, you could say Isaiah was a foul-mouthed individual, and so were the people! Perhaps that was why in His wisdom, God chose to send Isaiah—he knew the language of his people.

Since everyone on earth is a sinner, which sin disqualifies a person from holding the highest office in the land? On the scale of sinfulness, betrayal seems to me far worse than occasionally swearing "what the hell" as President Trump does. Why is a foul mouth worse to Max Lucado than a disloyal heart?

My pastoral guess is that Max Lucado is a product of his profession. He has built a successful career by writing on broadly-appealing topics. Being a pastor puts us in gatherings of some of the best human beings on earth. It's not like risking your life to preach the Gospel to Muslims. Or taking a stand for supernatural healing in an outdoor crusade and having a mob stampede 16 people to death—as happened in October 1999 to the late, great open-air evangelist Reinhard Bonnke.[10]

I have preached in the birthplace of voodoo, the Benin Republic, and had a mob of voodooists rock and reel our cars until we wondered whether our lives were endangered. If you don't preach the power of God and demonstrate that power in many parts of Africa, the people will not believe Jesus and the voodooists will eat you for lunch.

I've helped a crusade in Mandalay, Myanmar, where rebel forces with machine guns surrounded our stage to protect us from the police who often harassed Christians. The crusader was rough with people, rougher on the devil, and liked getting massages from Asian girls after the crusade was over (in public as far as I could tell). I don't imagine that such a Gospel preacher would be Max Lucado's cup of tea.

It's easy to criticize a rough-and-tough missionary while sitting in the pastorate of, say, San Antonio.[11] It's natural for an author of children's books to find such a missionary distasteful or brash. Yet the missionary got the job done. Hundreds came to Christ and villagers said they encountered Jesus in a way that they had never seen before. I learned to appreciate that God uses all different personalities to advance His kingdom. It's not my job to impose my personality preferences on other people's calls. Everybody should stay in their calling and be careful about venturing outside their anointing.

In the same way, most pastors have a gregarious nature and peace-loving personality, so Trump's personality would not naturally suit them. But Trump has a vastly different job description from theirs. Everyone has a personality to suit their calling. Let's not be too quick to judge another man's anointing.

The first disciples had a bad habit of looking for disqualifiers in other people. They proudly told Jesus they saw someone casting out devils in Jesus' Name and "we forbade him because he does not follow us." But Jesus was not impressed by their policing others. He responded, "Do not forbid him, for no one who works a miracle in My name can soon afterward speak evil of Me. For he who is not against us is on our side" (Mark 9:39-40).

It seems that the main argument "Never Trumper" Christians are making is that Donald Trump is a sinner; therefore, he cannot be President. How is this argument any different from the way the Pharisees spoke?

The Pharisees attempted to discredit Christ by accusing Him of sin! When Christ performed an undeniable work of healing a blind man, the Pharisees were infuriated by what this news would lead to. They tried to squash public enthusiasm for

Jesus by interrogating the man who was born blind, and yet he could see after meeting Jesus.

JOHN 9:24-25

24 So they again called the man who was blind, and said to him, "Give God the glory! We know that this Man is a SINNER." (This was their ad hominem attack, ignoring the good deed.)

25 He answered and said, "Whether He is a sinner or not I do not know. One thing I know: that though I was blind, now I see."

Notice the healed man ignored their accusation that Jesus was a sinner and pointed them to the good deed—his eyes were healed. The miraculous works should have convinced a God-fearing person that the accusations were spurious. The healed man's answer was in line with Jesus' teaching that we should judge a tree by its fruits (Matthew 7). But the Bible tells us that the Pharisees reviled him after they heard his answer. Listen to his second appeal to commonsense.

JOHN 9:30-33

30 The man answered and said to them, "Why, this is a marvelous thing, that you do not know where He is from; yet He has opened my eyes!

31 "Now we know that God does not hear sinners; but if anyone is a worshiper of God and does His will, He hears him.

32 "Since the world began it has been unheard of that anyone opened the eyes of one who was born blind.

33 "If this Man were not from God, He could do nothing."

I pray Christians come to see the same thing this once-blind man saw! Adopting his words, we can say, "This is a marvelous thing that you do not know where Trump is from; yet he fought for babies' right to be born, Christian hostages' right to be set free, pastors' right to preach without fear of government reprisal,[12] Jews' right to call Jerusalem their Eternal Capital, and many other good works you are about to read." One would think that the Pharisees would have no objection left against the once-blind man's faith in Jesus. What was their argument against the blind man?

JOHN 9:34

34 They answered and said to him, "You were completely born in sins, and are you teaching us?" And they cast him out.

The same argument being used today against Trump was used against both Jesus and the man he healed: we moral people don't support you because we know you're a sinner. John 9 is included in the Bible for such Christians to see.

God uses sinners, especially those who accept redemption. Would Max Lucado agree that God used Noah who was a drunk, Judah who had sex with his daughter-in-law, Rahab who was a prostitute, and David who was an adulterer? Judging people by their past rather than by their achievements seems to me an ungracious and un-Christian thing to do.[13]

God is using Donald Trump, who has a supernatural grace on him, to be a negotiator and an agent of justice. I have described on my YouTube channel[14] that he seems to be surrounded by an aura of protection that I call the "Trump Curse."[15] People who accuse him of crime get exposed or arrested for crime.[16] The journalists and Democrats who for years called him "deranged, unhinged, and mentally unfit," now have a presidential candidate who is truly senile, forgets his train of thought, and makes distasteful gaffes like, "If you have a problem figuring out whether you're for me or for Trump, then you ain't black."[17]

The Bible promises that when a guilty person calls down judgment, that judgment will come back on him.

PSALM 109:17 (ESV)

He loved to curse; let curses come upon him!

PSALM 27:2 (ESV)

When evildoers assail me to eat up my flesh, my adversaries and foes, it is they who stumble and fall.

This is called Divine Justice. I have watched holy justice protect me several times in my ministry. Three unrepentant accusers were arrested and charged for different crimes by the police. The Bible has many examples of divine protection surrounding a person who is accomplishing God's mission; he may not be perfect, but he cannot be eliminated till the mission is accomplished. I believe Trump is one of these persons.

If God could have used a born-again Christian pastor to lead the nation out of trouble, I believe He surely would have. Ted Cruz was not the man. I pray that Mike Pence will be that man. I pray that he is being groomed by Donald Trump to deal with the constant character assassination, drain the Washington swamp, and stand up to the real anti-Christs of the world: the Marxists and globalists who hate Christians.

To understand how God prepared Donald Trump for such a time of crisis as this, let's begin in 1946. Remember, the harmony of Scriptures will be our sure guide.

CHAPTER 3

PRE-PRESIDENTIAL TIMELINE: 1946-2016

June 14, 1946 — Donald John Trump was born in New York City on a total lunar eclipse, also known as a blood moon.[1]

LUKE 21:25 (ESV)

And there will be signs in sun and moon and stars, and on the earth distress of nations in perplexity because of the roaring of the sea and the waves,

May 14, 1948 — Israel became a nation, and was recognized by President Harry S. Truman,[2] 700 days after Trump's birth.[3]

ISAIAH 66:8

Who has heard such a thing? Who has seen such things? Shall the earth be made to give birth in one day? Or shall a nation be born at once? For as soon as Zion was in labor, She gave birth to her children.

April 27, 1961 — President John F. Kennedy made a speech at the Waldorf-Astoria Hotel which defined globalism and responsible news. The future President Trump would make similar statements (most notably at his Tulsa rally on June 21, 2020):

On Globalism: *"For we are opposed around the world by a monolithic and ruthless conspiracy that relies primarily on covert means for expanding its sphere of influence—on infiltration instead of invasion, on subversion instead of elections, on intimidation instead of free choice, on guerrillas by night instead of armies by day. It is a system which has conscripted vast human and material resources into the building of a tightly knit, highly efficient machine that combines military, diplomatic, intelligence, economic, scientific and political operations..."*

REVELATION 17:13 (ESV)

These are of one mind, and they hand over their power and authority to the beast.

On Responsible News: *"I have no intention of establishing a new Office of War Information to govern the flow of news. I am not suggesting any new forms of censorship or any new types of security classifications... But I am asking the members of the newspaper profession and the industry in this country to reexamine their own responsibilities, to consider the degree and the nature of the present danger, and to heed the duty of self-restraint which that danger imposes upon us all.*

"Every newspaper now asks itself, with respect to every story: 'Is it news?' All I suggest is that you add the question: 'Is it in the interest of the national security?'

"... I am not asking your newspapers to support the Administration, but I am asking your help in the tremendous task of informing and alerting the American people."[4]

JFK would be alive for only another 30 months. On November 22, 1963, he was assassinated—the fourth US president to become so in less than 100 years.[5]

It appeared that JFK tried to expose a wicked plot on a global scale. Conspiracies are hard to pin down and easy to deny. It is, by definition, a "secret plan" by a group to do something immoral or illegal. Encyclopedia Britannica said conspiracy as a crime is "perhaps the most amorphous area in Anglo-American criminal law."[6]

We do not need to look too far to see why some conspiracies circulate. No one has disproven the official story that Jeffrey Epstein killed himself. Yet no one I know believes that Jeffrey Epstein, the most wanted man on earth with connections to the most powerful people on earth, died by killing himself in a maximum-security prison while all cameras happened to stop recording and all security guards happened to be asleep. But the press can easily dismiss the skeptics by calling them a "conspiracy theorist."

I would agree that most conspiracy theories are far-fetched insults to the intellect. But it must also be said that the Bible teaches that secret plots are carried out by evil people in high places.

JEREMIAH 11:9 (NIV)

Then the Lord said to me, "There is a conspiracy among the people of Judah and those who live in Jerusalem.

2 SAMUEL 15:12-13 (ESV)

...And the conspiracy grew strong, and the people with Absalom kept increasing. And a messenger came to David, saying, "The hearts of the men of Israel have gone after Absalom."

ACTS 23:12-13 (NET)

When morning came, the Jews formed a conspiracy and bound themselves with an oath not to eat or drink anything

until they had killed Paul. There were more than forty of them who formed this conspiracy.

The balance is found in Isaiah 8:12 (NIV), "Do not call conspiracy everything this people calls a conspiracy; do not fear what they fear, and do not dread it."

We are not to be paranoid about every conspiracy theory on the Internet or social media. But we should perk up if a US President calls something a conspiracy, which is what JFK called global communism or "globalism" for short.

February 4, 1986 — a Georgia farmer named Lenard Dozier Hill III committed suicide after 3 years of bad crops in what some called the worst farm crisis since the Great Depression. He thought his life insurance would pay off his debts and save the farm that had been in the family for over a hundred years.

The insurance company didn't pay.

The property was in foreclosure when "a man from New York" stepped in to save the farm. Donald Trump called the family and told them that his wife Ivana had seen their story on the news and they wanted to help. Trump wrote the first check for $20,000 to stave off the foreclosure. He provided the last check of $78,000 to save the farm and invited the widow and her children to New York for a mortgage-burning ceremony two days before Christmas.

The daughter, Betsy Sharp, said, "We saw a whole different side of him that was kindhearted, to reach out to us, to help us. Most people don't know and see that side."[7]

Leonard Dozier Hill IV, the son, still lives on the farm.

COLOSSIANS 3:12 (NIV)

Therefore, as God's chosen people, holy and dearly loved, clothe yourselves with compassion, kindness, humility, gentleness and patience.

November 1, 1987 — *The Art of the Deal* by Donald J. Trump and journalist Tony Schwartz is released. The book reached number 1 on The New York Times Best Seller list and remained on the list for 51 non-consecutive weeks.

Author's note: my family developed real estate in New York and I remember every Cioccolanti had a copy of *The Art of the Deal* that Christmas. It made him a household name.

Later in August 2015 Trump said, "That's my second-favorite book of all time. Do you know what my first is? The Bible. Nothing beats the Bible. Nothing beats the Bible, not even *The Art of the Deal*, not even close."[8]

The American Presidency Project reports this story from 1995:

"Donald Trump was traveling along a New Jersey highway when the limo in which he was traveling experienced a flat tire. Spotting the disabled car along the side of the road, a passing motorist stopped to offer his assistance. After helping, Trump asked how he could repay the good Samaritan. The man asked that Trump send his wife a bouquet of flowers.

Trump agreed. True to his word, the bouquet arrived several weeks later along with a note saying, 'We've paid off your mortgage.'"[9]

This is one of many stories of Trump's generosity to strangers. They are difficult to verify because Trump himself rarely speaks of them.

Trump insisted on accepting blacks and Jews as members of his Mar-a-Lago Golf Club, at a time when other Palm Beach clubs still discriminated against minorities.

This won him the praise of Anti-Defamation League President Abraham Foxman who told the Wall Street Journal:

"He put the light on Palm Beach. Not on the beauty and the glitter, but on its seamier side of discrimination. It has an impact."[10]

Foxman credited Trump for motivating other clubs in Palm Beach to open up their membership to diversity.

Although Donald Trump speculated many times about running for president, notably for the 2004 and 2012 elections, the only time he ever ran before winning in 2016 was in 2000. It's important to include this episode as a baseline for Trump's vision for America and the White House.

Many politicians radically change their public persona when they run for office. (See the information on Harris below for an example.) Trump's current worldview seems to match his tone and tenor from 20 years ago.

Trump sought the nomination of the Reform Party for the 2000 presidential election. Even though he won his party's primaries in California and Michigan, he eventually dropped out. In his own opinion piece published by *The New York Times*, he wrote:

"I seriously thought that America might be ready for a businessman president, someone with an eye for the bottom line, someone who has created thousands of jobs and isn't part of the 'inside the Beltway' buddy system. I also thought that Americans might be ready for straight talk and that they would find an unscripted candidate appealing.

"Jesse Ventura's victory in Minnesota served as my model. A nonpolitician celebrity who spoke uncommonly straight to the voters, Mr. Ventura came out of nowhere to beat two experienced, big-name politicians at a time of economic prosperity, and he did so as the nominee of a fledgling third party.

"... A presidential exploratory campaign is the greatest civics lesson that a private citizen can have. In the course of my exploration, I met dozens of talented, dedicated Reform Party members who were involved, with little reward or recognition, solely because of their commitment to cleaning up the American political system...

"I also saw the underside of the Reform Party. The fringe element that wanted to repeal the federal income tax, believed that the country was being run by the Trilateral Commission and suspected

that my potential candidacy was a stalking horse for (take your pick) Gov. George W. Bush, Senator John McCain or Vice President Al Gore...

"In the days before I decided to end my presidential exploratory effort, I was watching CNN and saw Vice President Gore trudging through the snow in subzero temperatures, knocking on doors in New Hampshire—an obvious look of drudgery on his face. My experience was quite different. I had enormous fun thinking about a presidential candidacy and count it as one of my great life experiences."

"On why he left the Reform Party, he said, 'That is not the company I wish to keep.'"[11]

Donald Trump made a $10,000 donation to the West Bank settlement of Beit El in honor of his friend David Friedman whom he met in 1994. The two did not become friends until 2005, after Trump paid him a condolence call during his "sitting shiva"[12] for his father.[13] The donation was not known to the public till *The Washington Post* learned of it in January 2017, after Trump was elected President of the United States.[14]

Trump's love and support for Israel dates back a long time. After he became President, he appointed David Friedman as his ambassador to Israel.

January 22, 2005 — Donald Trump married Slovenian-American supermodel and businesswoman Melania Knauss. Their ceremony was performed according to Anglican rites at the Episcopal Church of Bethesda-by-the-Sea in Palm Beach, Florida.

October 25, 2009 — Ivanka Trump married Jared Kushner. Ivanka is the first daughter and second child of Donald Trump and Ivana Trump. She converted to Judaism in July 2009. She eats kosher and observes the Sabbath. Her husband was appointed Senior Advisor to the President on January 9, 2017.

April 12, 2011 — in an interview with David Brody of CBN, The Donald said: "I believe in God. I am Christian. I believe very strongly in God. I think the Bible is the Book, the thing. I was raised—and I gave you a picture just now, perhaps you'll use that picture, I found it from a long time ago, the First Presbyterian Church of Jamaica, Queens, that's where I went to church—I'm a Protestant. I'm a Presbyterian."

Interviewer: "Do you actively go to church?"

The Donald: "I go as much as I can. Always on Christmas. Always on Easter. Always when there's a major occasion. And during the Sundays—I'm a Sunday church person—I go when I can."

Interviewer: "I understand a lot of people send you Bibles. Is that true?"

The Donald: "Well I get sent Bibles by a lot of people." (Smiles.)

Interviewer: "Where are all those Bibles anyhow now?"

The Donald: "Well, we keep them in a certain place, a very nice place, but people send me Bibles. There's no way I'd do anything negative to a Bible, so what we do is we keep all of the Bibles—we just—I would have a fear of doing something other than very positive."

When asked about his views on babies and abortion, The Donald said:

"I'm pro-life, but I changed my view a number of years ago. One of the reasons I changed, one of the primary reasons, a friend of mine, his wife was pregnant, in this case married, and she was pregnant, and...he really didn't want the baby. He ends up having the baby and the baby is the apple of his eye. He says it's the greatest thing that's ever happened to him. And you know, here was a baby that wasn't going to be let into life. And I heard this and some other stories, and I am, I am pro-life...and I'll defend that."

Interviewer: "I know you're for traditional marriage, against gay marriage, what about civil union?"

The Donald: "To be honest with you, as far as civil union is concerned, I haven't totally formed my opinion. But there can be no discrimination against gays. I'm against gay marriage, which I took a lot of heat for that."

Interviewer: "Radical Islam is a huge issue in the country, but to Evangelicals...it's a big deal...You said on O'Reilly[15] actually there's a Muslim problem in this world. What do you mean by that exactly?"

The Donald: "Well, Bill O'Reilly asked me is there a Muslim problem, and I said, 'Absolutely, yes!' In fact, I went a step further and I said, 'I didn't see Swedish people knocking down the World Trade Center'... there's tremendous hatred out there that I've never seen anything like it."

The interviewer raised the "baggage" of his two failed marriages.

The Donald: "I'm a very hard worker. And I've always said it's very difficult for a woman to be married to me because I work. I work all the time."

Interviewer: "Is there a lesson you've learned in those two failed marriages?"

The Donald: "Well I think the lesson is—and they were both wonderful women—I think the message is that, you know, you do have to devote the requisite time to your marriage."[16]

It should be obvious to objective observers that Donald Trump raised exceptional children who are successful and represent him well. This was the only interview in which I heard him reveal his five prohibitions for his children: **no alcohol, no drugs, no smoking, no coffee** (for a time he said that), and **no tattoos.** Usually, he only mentions the first three.

Tony Perkins of the Family Research Council took note of Trump's answers and said: "Donald Trump is not talking like a typical politician. He's actually answering questions. And stepping out, he has made very clear he does not support same-sex marriage. He has said he's pro-life. And so that has gotten the attention of conservatives—social conservatives voters."[17]

February 26, 2013 — Basketball star Dennis Rodman made a visit to North Korea and met with the Chairman Kim Jong Un. Three months later, with a single tweet, he was able to motivate Kim to release an American prisoner, Kenneth Bae, who had been sentenced to 15 years hard labor. Kim released Bae one year later. Rodman said he encouraged President Obama to "pick up the phone and call" Kim, since both leaders were basketball fans.[18]

June 13, 2013 — Dennis Rodman returned to North Korea to meet their Olympic athletes and basketball players. He did not meet Kim Jong Un, but left gifts for the leader, including two signed basketball jerseys and a copy of Donald Trump's 1987 book *The Art of the Deal.*[19]

In July 2013, Rodman told Sports Illustrated: "My mission is to break the ice between hostile countries...I'll tell you this: If I don't finish in the top three for the next Nobel Peace Prize, something's seriously wrong."[20]

The press constantly mocked Rodman for going to North Korea, labelling him bizarre,[21] but in his unique style, Rodman paved the way for Trump's historic negotiations with Kim in June 2018, February 2019, and June 2019.

The path of Destiny is not a straight road.

October 18, 2013 — an Upstate New York bus driver named Darnell J. Barton stopped his bus on an Elmwood Avenue overpass because students in his bus spotted a woman hanging over the edge of the overpass. He got out of the bus and counseled the distraught woman not to commit suicide.

Donald Trump saw the story on the news and a month later wrote him a $10,000 check with a personal note:

"Although I know to you it was just a warm-hearted first response to a dangerous situation, your quick thinking resulted in a life being saved, and for that you should be rewarded."[22]

September 28, 2015 — Trump invited a group of Christian leaders to a two and a half hour meeting on the 26th floor of Trump Tower.[23] Included among them were Paula White, Kenneth and Gloria Copeland, Jan Crouch of TBN, Pastor Robert Jeffress of First Baptist Dallas, Pastor Darrell Scott of The New Spirit Revival Center in Cleveland, Pastor Mark Burns of Harvest Praise & Worship Center in South Carolina.[24]

Pastor Mark Burns later recalled the meeting to ABC News: "[Trump discussed] How people don't say Merry Christmas...he believes these are one of the core values that has made America great and we need to get back to those values. That was the beginning of what captivated my interest in Donald Trump. He's done business with literally almost every color and race, his work speaks volumes. I believe Donald Trump, not from what I've read in the paper, but in conversations, I've come to the conclusion that Trump has a personal relationship with God."[25]

March 14, 2016 — candidate Trump held a rally in Hickory, North Carolina, where he was introduced by African American Pastor Mark Burns. Pastor Burns had voted for Barack Obama and Bill Clinton, but he became convinced that Trump would defend Christian values. He stated:

"...we're about to elect a man in Donald Trump that believes in the name of Jesus Christ! And he is going to make sure we as Christians are protected when he gets to the White House!"

To ABC News Pastor Burns affirmed, "He's fighting for Christianity."[26]

March 31, 2016 — on the campaign trail in Wisconsin, Trump met a dying former Miss USA contestant, Miss Congeniality 2005, Melissa Young. She came to thank him personally because when she was in the hospital, Trump sent her handwritten cards and signed photos encouraging her to "stay brave! You're the strongest woman I know." Asked why she went to Trump's campaign rally, Ms. Young said:

"I was afraid that when my day comes, and I'm not here anymore, that I was never going to get a chance to thank him in person...he took the time to hear my words and ultimately leave the stage and come and hug me in the audience and he did make a promise that my son would be taken care of...he is the kindest man I have ever met. I think he has a heart of gold...he does so many things that he does not talk about like what he has done for my son."[27]

I had a revelation about this 2016 incident in Trump's life. Three things stood out to me:

1. **Trump's hyperbole** ("you're the strongest woman I know") **has been a part of his makeup.** Hyperboles are not meant to be taken at face value. When you say to your wife, "That was the best meal ever," you are not literally comparing all the meals you've ever had to hers. You probably have fond memories of your mother's cooking. You probably have enjoyed gourmet meals that could compare to your wife's. But what you mean to say is, "Honey, you're great, I love you, I appreciate the time you took to prepare this, and this meal hit the spot!" The media acts like it's never heard of hyperboles before and takes Trump to task for each positive statement delivered too glowingly. To Trump, he is being positive. When he titles a book, "Think Like a Billionaire," it is hyperbole. Virtually no one reading his book will ever have a billion dollars in their bank account. But Trump wants you to think like a huge success. Huge. He sincerely means it.
2. **This dying Miss Congeniality needed his hyperbole.** She did not need cold, calculated facts about how far the cancer had spread and how few

days she had left. She did not need to be reminded how bad she looked, how bad she felt, or how bad her dying days would be. She needed a kind person to lift up her chin and give her a nudge to live another day.

3. **This incident was one of those prophetic moments in life**—that's when something that happened in your past points to something much bigger in your future. America is the dying lady—spiritually dying to morality and God; literally dying with over 50 million babies aborted since 1973 and 623,500 young soldiers killed in America's endless wars since World War I.[28] America saw few friends left in the hospital room—the academics, intellectuals, communists, globalists, dictators and tyrants of the world all wanted her to fail. Then Trump walked into the room and handed her a card. With boundless optimism, he wrote, "The best is yet to come."

And America awoke to her destiny. America needs hyperbole. She has always been wooed by hyperbolic optimists. Jesus was fond of using hyperbole.

MATTHEW 17:20

So Jesus said to them, "...if you have faith as a mustard seed, you will say to this mountain, 'Move from here to there,' and it will move; and nothing will be impossible for you.

Jesus was unlike any other leader because His hyperboles will all come true.

May 24, 2016 — Donald Trump donated $1 million to the Marine Corps-Law Enforcement Foundation, which provides $30,000 scholarships to the children of Marines and federal law enforcement officers who die while on active duty.

Executive Director Sue Boulhosa said, "I'd never held a check that big before. We did a little dance, and then we ran downstairs to the bank and deposited it." The check signed by Trump was one of a dozen he donated in 2016 to veteran charities, totaling more than $5.6 million.[29]

PROVERBS 11:25 (NIV)

A generous person will prosper; whoever refreshes others will be refreshed.

May 31, 2016 — Andy Biggio, the founder of New England Wounded Veterans, received a check for $75,000 signed by Donald Trump. He said, "I pretty much screamed my head off for 10 minutes."[30]

Mr. Biggio is a Marine veteran who served tours in Iraq and Afghanistan. When he came home, he started his charity to help military families. How did New England Wounded Veterans end up on Trump's radar screen? CBS Boston reported:

"When Andy served in Iraq, he fought alongside a fellow Marine was named Joe Schiller, from New York. When they got home from war, Joe followed Andy's charity on Facebook. One-day Joe called Andy and told him that his father was Donald Trump's bodyguard. Joe suggested to Trump that Andy's organization was worthy of a donation."[31]

June 21, 2016 — candidate Trump held a closed-door meeting at a hotel in Times Square to answer questions from evangelicals and Catholic conservatives. Christian Governor Mike Huckabee, a former Baptist pastor, was the moderator. He said he had seen Trump up close. "People can fake it on stage, they can walk out and do the happy family moment, but you can't fake that backstage."[32]

THE DONALD: “I have great children...Through God they were born intelligent, they all went to great colleges.” He noted, as he often does, that he told his children: no alcohol, no drugs and no smoking. He didn’t mention that he’d taught them all by example, and by having them do hard work, just as he learned his business from his father.

Franklin Graham closed the meeting by reminding Christians that God used flawed people in the Bible. Moses murdered an Egyptian. David committed adultery. Peter denied Jesus three times. “There is none of us that are perfect. There’s no perfect person — there’s only one, and that’s the Lord Jesus Christ, but he’s not running for president of the United States.”[33]

July 15, 2016 — candidate Trump selected as his Vice Presidential running mate Mike Pence, a born-again Christian and the 50th Governor of Indiana (2013-2017).

The prophetic implication of this will be seen in 2024 when I expect Mr. Pence to run for President... and win.

NEHEMIAH 7:2 (NIV)

I put in charge of Jerusalem my brother Hanani, along with Hananiah the commander of the citadel, because he was a MAN of INTEGRITY and feared God more than most people do.

September 11, 2016 — African American Pastor Darrell Scott in Cleveland, Ohio did a pre-church service interview in which he came out and supported candidate Trump: “I like him. I think he’s a great leader. And I think he’d be a good President...He’s a man’s man, and that’s what I like about him. You know, he reminds me of me. He’s a white me. (Laughs.)”[34]

Pastor Scott had a chance to speak to The Donald directly and here was his impression on whether Trump is a racist: “I know he’s not a racist. I mean I was convinced on that first day from that first conversation. The reason I was convinced was because he did not go overboard trying to convince me he was NOT a racist. I was waiting on him to give me some stock answers like, 'I had a black friend when I was growing up' or 'our maid used to be black' or 'I knew a black guy once.' I was waiting for that and he didn't do it, it (race) was a non-issue to him."[35]

He concluded the interview: "The title of President is Chief Executive Officer of the United States of America. I think he'd be an excellent CEO of the country."[36]

* * * † * * *

IN POLITICS, CONTRADICTIONS ARE THE NORM

CONSISTENCY IS hard to maintain in anyone's life. Politicians' lives, in particular, are riddled with contradictions. One recent illustration will suffice for the purpose of this book.

Kamala Harris, the 2020 VP candidate for the Democrat Party, is an example of contradictions. In 2014, Harris called 18 to 24 year olds "stupid";[37] in 2019 she called for the voting age to be lowered to 16 and wanted young people to get out there and vote.[38] When asked later whether she wanted to lower the voting age to 16, she gave a non-answer, "I'm really interested in having that conversation."[39] That's political speak for "you caught me." People trained in law are particularly adept at deflecting and diverting away direct questions.

As district attorney of San Francisco and attorney general of California, Kamala Harris was the state's "top cop," playing her part in a system that incarcerated blacks at a rate 12 times higher than whites.[40] She failed to hold police accountable in misconduct cases and did not support body cameras for police. She advocated for wrongfully convicted people, like death row inmate Kevin Cooper, to stay behind bars and be executed. In the words of University of San Francisco associate law professor Lara Bazelon, "Ms. Harris fought tooth and nail to uphold wrongful convictions that had been secured through official misconduct that included evidence tampering, false testimony and the suppression of crucial information by prosecutors."[41]

But in 2020, Kamala Harris turned over a new leaf. She claims that she fights hard for black people, for criminal justice reform, and that she wants to defund the police—a goal of Antifa and Black Lives Matter.

The media is complicit in spinning the narrative to promote or destroy a political candidate. In 2016, the headlines read, "Kamala Harris becomes first Indian-American US senator."[42] In 2020, the headlines read, "Kamala Harris makes history as first black woman VP nominee[43]." (The claim is untrue.)[44] So which is it—Asian American or African American?

Harris' father is Jamaican, a descendant of an Irish slave owner named Hamilton Brown. Harris' mother is Tamil Indian and she claimed her Indian family shaped her values. However, in the age of Black Lives Matter, her Tamil roots have been underplayed and she is presented as a black candidate to appeal to black voters.

If Trump had made any of these self-contradictory claims, the media would have called him a liar. But how does the media spin the narrative for a Democrat candidate? Listen to CNN's explanation:

CNN wrote that Kamala Harris has a "long and complex record as district attorney of San Francisco and attorney general of California."[45] When someone comes to me for pastoral counseling and does not want to tell me the full truth, they tend to tell me, "It's complicated." While in some context it is appropriate to avoid complicated matters, a counseling session is not one of them...nor is a journalistic evaluation of a VP candidate.

The purpose of including some pre-Presidential highlights

is to give a baseline for how Mr. Trump has been before entering politics. It is fair to say that he has not been perfectly consistent. Some views evolved, some views stayed the same, and he completely flipped on abortion. However, it would not be fair to say he lied about his core beliefs or contradicted any of his political positions for expediency over the past 20 years.

CHAPTER 4

FIRST YEAR: 2017

HISTORICALLY, US presidents have been judged on their first 100 days in office. Therefore this chapter covering Trump's first 100 days (and beyond) will set the pace for the rest of the presidency.

January 20, 2017 — Day 1. Donald J. Trump became President of the United States at the age of 70 years, 7 months, 7 days.

Seven is a pattern in Trump's life. It is also a hallmark of God's handiwork.

> JOSHUA 6:4
>
> **And SEVEN priests shall bear SEVEN trumpets of rams' horns before the ark. But the SEVENTH day you shall march around the city SEVEN times, and the priests shall blow the trumpets.**

January 20, 2017 — It was revealed that President Trump had given $10,000 to a single dad named Shane Bouvet to help him with his father battling cancer. He also gave the young man a VIP ticket to the Presidential Inauguration.

In an interview with Fox Business, Mr. Bouvet said,

"Donald Trump is the most genuine, humble, caring person I've ever met in my life...he did a lot for my dad who's battling cancer...he spoke with my dad and wow my dad was so happy...like I said, when I met Donald Trump I felt God's Presence in that tent, I really did."[1]

1 PETER 3:8 (CSB)

Finally, all of you be like-minded and sympathetic, love one another, and be compassionate and humble,

January 23, 2017 — President Trump reinstated the "Mexico City Policy," which bans federal money from going to foreign organizations that perform abortions, provide information on abortion, or perform involuntary sterilizations.[2] Democrats call federal funding of these NGOs "assistance for voluntary population planning."[3]

The Mexico City Policy has been enforced by every Republican president and suspended by every Democrat president after inauguration.

- Bill Clinton rescinded the policy on January 22, 1993.
- George W. Bush reinstated it on January 22, 2001.
- Barack Obama rescinded it on January 23, 2009.
- Donald Trump reinstated it on January 23, 2017.

PSALM 139:13-14 (NIV)

13 For you created my inmost being; you knit me together in my mother's womb.

14 I praise you because I am fearfully and wonderfully made...

January 24, 2017 — President Donald J. Trump signed a series of Executive Orders and Presidential Memoranda to reduce regulations and expedite high priority energy and infrastructure projects, including the Keystone XL Pipeline and Dakota Access Pipelines.

The Keystone XL Pipeline is a 1,100-mile crude oil pipeline to connect oil production in Alberta, Canada to refineries in the United States. The Dakota Access Pipeline is the pipeline to carry 500,000 barrels of crude oil per day from North Dakota to oil markets in the US.[4]

Little did anyone know that President Trump's action within his first week in office would be led by the Lord and have significant prophetic implications only three years later. The Peace Agreement between Israel and the UAE (with Bahrain soon to follow)[5] would have been unlikely without America first becoming energy independent.

"Independence" does not mean America no longer buys different kinds of oil from abroad, or that America single-handedly controls the price of a commodity. Oil is globally traded, comes in many forms, and many factors affect the price of oil. Independence does mean America will become the largest producer of energy and that the Middle East will lose a bargaining chip when negotiating with President Trump. (Read what happens in August 2020.)

PSALM 24:1 (KJV)

The earth is the Lord's, and the fulness thereof; the world, and they that dwell therein.

January 25, 2017 — President Trump issued an Executive Order "Enhancing Public Safety in the Interior of the United States," reestablishing law and order in immigration policy. He also established the "Victims of Immigration Crime Engagement" (VOICE), which is a government agency within the Department of Homeland Security.

THE PRESIDENT: *"Many aliens who illegally enter the United States and those who overstay or otherwise violate the terms of their visas present a significant threat to national security and public safety... Sanctuary jurisdictions across the United States willfully violate Federal law in an attempt to shield aliens from removal from the United States. These jurisdictions have caused immeasurable harm to the American people and to the very fabric of our Republic... It is the policy of the executive branch to... Ensure the faithful execution of the immigration laws of the United States... against all removable aliens."*[6]

This change in executive policy led to the hiring of 10,000 additional ICE agents and 5,000 additional Border Patrol agents, 40% more "enforcement and removal operations"[7] than compared to President Obama's last year.

PSALM 122:7

Peace be within YOUR WALLS, Prosperity within your palaces.

January 30, 2017 — President Trump issued an Executive Order on Reducing Regulation and Controlling Regulatory Costs.

THE PRESIDENT: *"It is the policy of the executive branch to be prudent and financially responsible in the expenditure of funds... Toward that end, it is important that for every one new regulation issued, at least two prior regulations be identified for elimination, and that the cost of planned regulations be prudently managed and controlled through a budgeting process."*[8]

By July 2020, it was estimated that federal agencies had taken more than 7 deregulatory actions for every significant regulatory action. The President proclaimed: "We've begun the most far-reaching regulatory reform in American history."[9]

MARK 10:42-43 (ESV)

42 (Jesus said) **"You know that those who are considered**

rulers of the Gentiles lord it over them, and their great ones exercise authority over them.

43 "But it shall not be so among you. But whoever would be great among you must be your servant,"

January 31, 2017 — President Trump nominated his first pro-life judge to the United States Supreme Court, Justice Neil Gorsuch.[10]

For Christians, this is one of the biggest campaign promises kept within less than two weeks in office. It will not be his last action for infant life protection.

Promise made; promise kept.

LEVITICUS 18:21 (NIV)

Do not give any of your children to be sacrificed to Molek, for you must not profane the name of your God. I am the LORD.

PSALM 37:28

For the Lord LOVES justice...

February 7, 2017 — Trump's appointee for Secretary of Education, born again Christian billionaire Betsy Devos, was confirmed by the Senate by a 51–50 margin, with Vice President Mike Pence breaking the tie in her favor. She was nominated by the Trump transition team as early as November 23, 2016, but she was not a favorite pick of teachers' unions as she is one of the leading advocates for greater school choice. Her confirmation became a landmark spiritually and politically, as this was the first time in US history that a Cabinet nominee's confirmation was decided by the Vice President's tie-breaking vote.[11] Her being at the helm of the Department of Education has resulted in "rising support for charter schools, taxpayer-funded vouchers, and tax credits for private-school vouchers, programs aimed at expanding options for parents looking beyond traditional public schools as she brings attention to them."[12]

PROVERBS 22:6

Train up a child in the way he should go, And when he is old he will not depart from it.

2 TIMOTHY 4:3 (ESV)

For the time is coming when people will not endure sound teaching, but having itching ears they will accumulate for themselves teachers to suit their own passions,

February 7, 2017 — President Trump saved America over $700 Million Dollars on F-35 Fighter Jets.

CNN: *"Defense giant Lockheed Martin has agreed to sell 90 new F-35 fighter jets to the US Defense Department for $8.5 billion—a deal that amounts to more than $700 million in savings over the last batch of aircraft delivered... Lockheed Martin CEO Marillyn Hewson gave then-President-elect Trump her "personal commitment" to cut the cost of the stealthy F-35 fighter jet after Trump posted a tweet criticizing the program..."*[13]

PROVERBS 28:16 (NIV)

A tyrannical ruler practices extortion, but one who hates ill-gotten gain will enjoy a long reign.

PROVERBS 22:16 (ESV)

Whoever oppresses the poor to increase his own wealth, or gives to the rich, will only come to poverty.

February 22, 2017 — President Trump directed the Department of Education (DOE) and the Department of Justice

(DOJ) to revoke Obama's transgender bathroom policy, which allowed school children who claimed to be "transgender" to access restrooms, locker rooms, and showers of their choosing.[14]

This was not Trump's unilateral decision, but a response to the US Court of Appeals for the Fourth Circuit finding that the use of the term "sex" in Obama's regulations was ambiguous and "novel," because it implied that "biological sex" could change or be changed. Meanwhile, a federal district court in Texas issued a ruling maintaining that the term "sex" unambiguously refers to "biological sex."

The DOE and DOJ noted that the withdrawal "does not leave students without protections from discrimination, bullying, or harassment. All schools must ensure that all students, including LGBT students, are able to learn and thrive in a safe environment."[15]

GENESIS 5:2 (ESV)

Male and female he created them, and he blessed them and named them Man when they were created.

February 28, 2017 — President Trump signed the HBCU Executive Order, establishing the White House Initiative on Historically Black Colleges and Universities (HBCU).

This moved the federal initiative to assist HBCUs from the Department of Education into the Executive Office of the President.

THE PRESIDENT: *"With this executive order, we will make HBCUs a priority in the White House — an absolute priority...And we will pledge our support to you, your mission, and to our shared mission of bringing education and opportunity to all of our people."*[16]

Johnny C. Taylor, president and CEO of the Thurgood Marshall College Fund, was one of several African American leaders present in the Oval Office during the signing. He made the following observation:

"This was something that, frankly, the black college community assumed would have been easily accomplished with the first African-American president, and after over eight years of repeated requests, to think that within 45 days of his presidency we were able to convene all of the [HBCU] presidents in the Oval Office [Monday] and [on Tuesday] a subset of us were able to come back and sign the executive order the same day that the [president] is preparing for first State of the Union address. [That] gives this tremendous importance. It's bittersweet, but at the end of the day, we focus on the sweet."[17]

Trump would make good on this initiative by giving more money to HBCUs than any other president.[18] This achievement so early in his presidency was significant for two reason: 1) it flies in the face of the media's incessant smears that he is racist; 2) America had its first black American president for 8 years, but it took Trump only a year to give more funding to black universities than Obama did.

1 JOHN 3:17-18

17 But whoever has this world's goods, and sees his brother in need, and shuts up his heart from him, how does the love of God abide in him?

18 My little children, let us not love in word or in tongue, but in deed and in truth.

March 4, 2017 — Day 44 of Trump's first term.[19] Trump revealed via tweets that he had learned Obama had wire tapped Trump Tower and tapped his phones. He compared Obama's surveillance to Nixon's scandal in Watergate.[20]

PSALM 119:23 (ESV)

Even though princes sit plotting against me, your servant will meditate on your statutes.

I have found in ministry that when God favors you, He will expose the scams and lies that your enemies try to hide. The Lord sees the truth.

PSALM 69:4

Those who hate me without a cause Are more than the hairs of my head; They are mighty who would destroy me, Being my enemies wrongfully; Though I have stolen nothing, I still must restore it.

Joseph was hated by his brothers without cause. David was hated by his brothers without cause. Jesus was hated by His own people without cause. In all three cases, the jealous brothers were demoted and the chosen brother was promoted by God.

GENESIS 12:3 (ESV)

I will bless those who bless you, and him who dishonors you I will curse, and in you all the families of the earth shall be blessed."

March 7, 2017 — Trump's choice for Secretary of Housing and Urban Development (HUD), world-renowned neurosurgeon Dr. Ben Carson, was confirmed by the Senate by a vote of 58–41.[21]

Although baptized as a Seventh Day Adventist, Dr. Carson has been an inter-denominational attendee and guest speaker. He said in 1999, "I spend just as much time in non-Seventh-day Adventist churches because I'm not convinced that the denomination is the most important thing. I think it's the relationship with God that's most important."[22]

EXODUS 18:21 (NIV)

But select capable men from all the people--men who

fear God, trustworthy men who hate dishonest gain—and appoint them as officials over thousands, hundreds, fifties and tens.

April 6, 2017 — Day 77 of Trump's first term. A prophecy continued to unfold in Syria. President Trump initiated a missile strike on a Syrian airbase in response to an alleged chemical weapons attack in Syria that left at least 86 civilians dead.[23] The Bible predicts the utter destruction of Syria's capital in the end times.

ISAIAH 17:1

The burden against Damascus. "Behold, Damascus will cease from being a city, And it will be a ruinous heap."

The setting of this is in the end times when there will be 1) a recognition of the state of Israel and 2) a return to the God of Israel, the Creator of the Universe.

ISAIAH 17:7

In that day a man will look to his Maker, And his eyes will have respect for the Holy One of Israel.

April 7, 2017 — Neil Gorsuch was confirmed to the Supreme Court, replacing the seat made vacant by the sudden death of Ronald Reagan's appointee Justice Antonin Scalia.

Scalia was the most prominent Originalist judge of his time. An Originalist holds the view that the Constitution cannot be a malleable "living document" subject to change. Many countries in the world have existed without a constitution. The Founding Fathers designed a US Constitution so that any law could be changed by Congress or the States *except* those in the Constitution. They are unchangeable except by a Constitutional Amendment. To Scalia, "judicial activism" made a mockery of the US Constitution by attempting to transfer the power to make legal changes from the legislature to the judiciary.

DANIEL 6:8

Now, O king, establish the decree and sign the writing, so that it cannot be changed, according to the law of the Medes and Persians, which does not alter.

MALACHI 3:6 (KJV)

For I am the Lord, I change not; therefore ye sons of Jacob are not consumed.

April 13, 2017 — President Trump ordered the US military to drop the "Mother of All Bombs (MOAB)," the largest non-nuclear bomb ever used in combat, on ISIS targets hiding in caves in Afghanistan. At least 94 terrorists were killed.[24]

2 SAMUEL 2:38

I have pursued my enemies and destroyed them...

ISAIAH 14:5

The Lord has broken the staff of the wicked, The scepter of the rulers;

April 28, 2017 — Day 99. President Donald J. Trump proclaimed May 2017 as Jewish American Heritage Month.[25]

EXODUS 19:5-6 (ESV)

5 Now therefore, if you will indeed obey my voice and keep my covenant, you shall be my treasured possession among all peoples, for all the earth is mine;

6 and you shall be to me a kingdom of priests and a holy

nation. These are the words that you shall speak to the people of Israel.

President Trump also signed an Executive Order to lift bans on offshore drilling in the Atlantic and Arctic Oceans put in place by former President Barack Obama.

THE PRESIDENT: *"Our country is blessed with incredible natural resources, including abundant offshore oil and natural gas reserves. But the federal government has kept 94 percent of these offshore areas closed for exploration and production...This deprives our country of potentially thousands and thousands of jobs and billions of dollars in wealth.*

"This executive order starts the process of opening offshore areas to job-creating energy exploration. It reverses the previous administration's Arctic leasing ban. So hear that: It reverses the previous administration's Arctic leasing ban, and directs Secretary Zinke to allow responsible development of offshore areas that will bring revenue to our Treasury and jobs to our workers.

"Finally, this order will enable better scientific study of our offshore resources and research that has blocked everything from happening for far too long. You notice it doesn't get blocked for other nations. It only gets blocked for our nation. Renewed offshore energy production will reduce the cost of energy, create countless good jobs, and make America more secure and far more energy independent."[26]

DEUTERONOMY 33:24 (Jacob's blessing on and prophecy to his sons)

And of Asher he said: "Asher is most blessed of sons; Let him be favored by his brothers, And let him dip his foot in oil."

When God said He would favor Asher, He said he would be rich in oil. In ancient times, an abundance of olive oil was a symbol of the good life. Today, oil still symbolizes God's blessing on a nation, and both Israel and America will find more of it to provide energy.

April 29, 2017 — The first 100 days were completed on Saturday, a Sabbath or rest day. Nothing eventful happened.

The President had made ambitious goals during his campaign. In a statement released on Friday, a day ahead of the milestone, the President said:

"I truly believe that the first 100 days of my Administration has been just about the most successful in our country's history. In just fourteen weeks, my administration has brought profound change to Washington...

"My Administration is the first in the modern political era to confirm a new Supreme Court Justice in the first 100 days–the last time it happened was 136 years ago in 1881...

"The White House is once again the People's House. And I will do everything in my power to be the People's President..."[27]

May 4, 2017 — President Trump issued an Executive Order "Promoting Free Speech and Religious Liberty."

THE PRESIDENT: *"It shall be the policy of the executive branch to vigorously enforce Federal law's robust protections for religious freedom. The Founders envisioned a Nation in which religious voices and views were integral to a vibrant public square, and in which religious people and institutions were free to practice their faith without fear of discrimination or retaliation by the Federal Government."*[28]

JOHN 8:32

And you shall know the truth, and the truth shall make you free."

May 4, 2017 — President Donald J. Trump proclaimed May 4, 2017 as a National Day of Prayer.[29]

THE PRESIDENT: *"We come together on our National Day of Prayer as one Nation, under God, to show gratitude for our many blessings...We are also reminded and reaffirm that all human beings have the right, not only to pray and worship according to their consciences, but to practice their faith in their homes, schools, charities, and businesses in private and in the public square free from government coercion, discrimination, or persecution.* ***Religion is not merely an intellectual exercise, but also a practical one that demands action in the world.*** *Even the many prisoners around the world who are persecuted for their faith can pray privately in their cells.* ***But our Constitution demands more: the freedom to practice one's faith publicly.***

"The religious liberty guaranteed by the Constitution is not a favor from the government, but a natural right bestowed by God... As Thomas Jefferson wisely questioned: 'Can the liberties of a nation be thought secure when we have removed their only firm basis, a conviction in the minds of the people that these liberties are the gift of God?'"[30]

1 TIMOTHY 2:1-4 (ESV)

1 First of all, then, I urge that supplications, prayers, intercessions, and thanksgivings be made for all people,

2 for kings and all who are in high positions, that we may lead a peaceful and quiet life, godly and dignified in every way.

3 This is good, and it is pleasing in the sight of God our Savior,

4 who desires all people to be saved and to come to the knowledge of the truth.

May 22, 2017 — Donald Trump became the first sitting US president to visit and pray at the Western Wall, the only remnant of the Second Temple Jesus preached at and predicted would be destroyed.

The Western Wall is significant to both Christians and Jews. For Christians, it is a vindication of one of the New Testament predictions made by Yeshua or Jesus. He said in AD 33 the Temple would be destroyed. He warned those who saw the signs He gave to flee. In AD 70, Roman General Titus destroyed the Temple and the city.

Historically, **no Christian died in the sack of Jerusalem because all of them believed Jesus' warning and acted on it.** They fled to safety as instructed by the Lord as soon as they saw the city surrounded. In the last generation, Jesus instructed Jews to do the same as soon as they see the "abomination of desolation" sitting inside the Third Temple.

The "Temple question"—that is, when would it be destroyed—is central to Christian eschatology. The disciples' question sparked the most famous end time sermon by Yeshua (Matthew 24, Mark 13, Luke 21), who listed end time signs clearly and sequentially.

> MATTHEW 24:1-2
>
> **1 Then Jesus went out and departed from the temple, and His disciples came up to show Him the buildings of the temple.**
>
> **2 And Jesus said to them, "Do you not see all these things? Assuredly, I say to you, NOT ONE STONE shall be left here upon another, that shall not be thrown down."**

The stones Jesus was referring to were the stones of the Second Temple. They are all gone. What remains is the retaining wall King Herod the Great built. Since the western side of this wall is presumed to be the closest to the original Holy of Holies, it has become the holiest site in Judaism.

Left without the Temple, Jews can no longer fulfill some of the Mosaic laws, one of which requires a yearly sacrifice on the Day of Atonement by the High Priest inside the Holy of Holies. Rabbinic or Talmudic Judaism has replaced this requirement with man-made penance and good works, but that bypasses the point God is making. The absence of a Temple is supposed to remind all Torah observant Jews that sin can only be paid for by blood, and after the Messiah's blood sacrifice in AD 33, this sacred object lesson was no longer needed. Torah observers were to put their trust in the sinless blood of Yeshua HaMashiach to atone for all sins—Jews' and Gentiles'.

The fact that Donald Trump became the first sitting President to pray at this site is a special honor from the Lord.

June 1, 2017 — President Donald J. Trump formally withdrew from the Paris Climate Accord.[31]

In my book *Trump's Unfinished Business*, chapter 12, "Climate Change Religion," I exposed many lies propagated by Global Warming/ Climate Change alarmists. They blamed the Australian Bush Fires of 2019-2020 on Australia not doing more to comply with the Paris Climate Accord; yet 1) bushfires are an annual occurrence pre-dating the arrival of whites to Australia, and 2) many of those who love the Paris Climate Accord don't even know what's in it. Read this one chapter in *Trump's Unfinished Business* to understand why it is a scientific farce and a globalist agenda to centralize political power, not change the earth's weather.

THE PRESIDENT: *"As someone who cares deeply about the environment, which I do, I cannot in good conscience support a deal that punishes the United States—which is what it does–the world's leader in environmental protection, while imposing no meaningful obligations on the world's leading polluters.*

"For example, under the agreement, China will be able to increase these emissions by a staggering number of years—13. They can do whatever they want for 13 years. Not us. India makes its participation contingent on receiving billions and billions and billions of dollars in foreign aid from developed countries. There are many other examples. But the bottom line is that the Paris Accord is very unfair, at the highest level, to the United States.

"... the current agreement effectively blocks the development of

clean coal in America... China will be allowed to build hundreds of additional coal plants. So we can't build the plants, but they can, according to this agreement. India will be allowed to double its coal production by 2020. Think of it: India can double their coal production. We're supposed to get rid of ours. Even Europe is allowed to continue construction of coal plants.

"In short, the agreement doesn't eliminate coal jobs, it just transfers those jobs out of America and the United States and ships them to foreign countries.

"This agreement is less about the climate and more about other countries gaining a financial advantage over the United States.

"... Even if the Paris Agreement were implemented in full, with total compliance from all nations, it is estimated it would only produce a two-tenths of one degree — think of that; this much — Celsius reduction in global temperature by the year 2100. Tiny, tiny amount. In fact, 14 days of carbon emissions from China alone would... totally wipe out the gains from America's expected reductions in the year 2030.

"... The Paris Agreement handicaps the United States economy in order to win praise from the very foreign capitals and global activists that have long sought to gain wealth at our country's expense. They don't put America first. I do, and I always will."[32]

In a few short words, President Trump showed his understanding of the alarmists' ulterior motives: global redistribution of power and wealth away from America. It is Climate Marxism. I go so far as to call it "Climate Terrorism" in my book *Trump's Unfinished Business*, with evidence as to why.

THE WHITE HOUSE: "*... the President vowed that the US would maintain its position as a world leader in clean energy, while protecting the economy and strengthening the work force.*

"The Paris Climate Accord cost the US economy nearly $3 trillion in reduced output, over 6 million industrial jobs, and over 3 million manufacturing jobs.

"Today's announcement is yet another example of the President's commitment to put America and its workers first."[33]

America's greatest threat is globalist fanatics who want to destroy America and replace it with global governance. Trump's withdrawal from the Paris Climate Accord was the first blow to globalism. It was a signal to globalists that he would not bow at their command or yield America's treasure to them. Although many people will not take the time to understand the true nature of the Paris Climate Accord and the positive effects of withdrawing from it, it will, in my view, go down as one of the great achievements of the Trump presidency.

The globalists wooed Trump by inviting him to speak at Davos (officially the "World Economic Forum Annual Meeting") on January 28, 2018. His message to them, contrary to what they expected, was a resounding rejection of globalism. (You will find it in the next chapter.)

NUMBERS 35:33 (ESV)

You shall not pollute the land in which you live, for blood pollutes the land, and no atonement can be made for the land for the blood that is shed in it...

God is against pollution, and the dirtiest pollution in our land is the shedding of innocent blood—both abortion and pedophilia top the list. Ridding ourselves of both would be **the most responsible action for the planet.** The effects will be felt and seen by all life on earth. Everybody loves to live in a clean place.

July 21, 2017 — President Trump issued a Statement on American Citizens Unjustly Detained in Iran.

WHITE HOUSE: *"President Donald J. Trump and his Administration are redoubling efforts to bring home all Americans unjustly detained abroad. The United States condemns hostage takers and nations that continue to take hostages and detain our citizens without just cause or due process."*[34]

ISAIAH 61:1 (NIV)

The Spirit of the Sovereign LORD is on me, because the LORD has anointed me to proclaim good news to the poor. He has sent me to bind up the brokenhearted, to proclaim freedom for the captives and release from darkness for the prisoners,

August 25, 2017 — President Trump issued an Executive Order Imposing Sanctions with Respect to the Situation in Venezuela.[35]

Venezuela is a country blessed with natural resources, especially oil. While the rest of the world was struggling to recover from World War II, Venezuela had the fourth-richest GDP per capita on earth by 1950. It was 2x richer than Chile, 4x richer than Japan, and 12x richer than China![36]

With free-market capitalism, Venezuela grew into the richest nation in Latin America. This economic growth reversed and collapsed after the 1998 election of socialist Hugo Chávez, who promised to redistribute the country's energy wealth to reduce poverty.

Today the Venezuelan currency is hyper-inflated to the degree that no one picks it up when thrown on the streets. The country has massive shortages of food, electricity, and other essential goods, and escalating violence in its capital.[37]

This is what socialism does to a nation. It steals the wealth of honest, productive people and puts it in the hands of corrupt, unproductive politicians.

EXODUS 20:15 (KJV)

Thou shalt not steal.

August 31, 2017 — President Trump pledged $1 million of his own personal money to aid the victims of Hurricane Harvey in Texas and Louisiana. He took 4 months to fulfill his promise. Harvey is tied with Katrina as the costliest hurricane in US history.[38]

September 5, 2017 — President Trump restored responsibility and the rule of law to immigration (revoked DACA).

At his first State of the Union Address on February 28, 2017, the President mapped out his agenda, "I believe that real and positive immigration reform is possible, as long as we focus on the following goals: To improve jobs and wages for Americans; to strengthen our nation's security; and to restore respect for our laws."[39]

The White House issued the following: *"Responsibly Ending Unlawful Immigration Policy: Today, the Trump Administration is rescinding the previous Administration's memorandum creating the unlawful Deferred Action for Childhood Arrivals (DACA) program and has begun to end the program responsibly...*

"The DACA program was never intended to be permanent—even President Obama admitted it was a temporary, extraordinary measure. And President Obama repeatedly recognized that such unilateral actions were in excess of the Executive's appropriate role.

"President Obama admitted publicly on at least 22 occasions that creating a DACA-like program was beyond his authority. President Obama said:

"In 2011, that 'there are enough laws on the books by Congress that are very clear in terms of how we have to enforce our immigration system that for me to simply through Executive order ignore those congressional mandates would not conform with my appropriate role as President.'"[40]

ISAIAH 62:8-9

...never again will foreigners drink the new wine for

which you have toiled; but those who harvest it will eat it and praise the Lord...

The Lord is pro-immigration and anti-invasion. This verse implies that because Americans ate and forgot to praise the Lord, the door was open for illegal immigrants to come in and drink from the teats of the Welfare State.

September 8, 2017 — President Trump proclaimed Friday, September 8, 2017, through Sunday, September 10, 2017, as National Days of Prayer and Remembrance.

THE PRESIDENT: *"During National Days of Prayer and Remembrance, our Nation recalls the nearly 3,000 innocent people murdered on September 11, 2001... We also pause to pray for those who fight today and every day to protect our country from terrorism. Those who commit acts of terror only have power if we choose to fear."*[41]

LUKE 13:4-5

4 "Or those eighteen on whom the TOWER IN SILOAM FELL and KILLED them, do you think that they were worse sinners than all other men who dwelt in Jerusalem?

5 "I tell you, no; but unless you repent you will all likewise perish."

October 7, 2017 — Under instruction by the President, Attorney General Jeff Sessions issued a Department of Justice Memorandum detailing how federal departments and agencies are to interpret religious liberty protections in federal law.

THE DEPARTMENT OF JUSTICE: *"Religious liberty is not merely a right to personal religious beliefs or even to worship in a sacred place. It also encompasses religious observance and practice. Except in the narrowest circumstances, no one should be forced to choose between living out his or her faith and complying with the law... The following twenty principles should guide administrative agencies and executive departments in carrying out this task."*[42]

I will list only half for you to see how strongly-worded this DOJ memorandum is.

1. The freedom of religion is a fundamental right of paramount importance, expressly protected by federal law.

2. The free exercise of religion includes the right to act or abstain from action in accordance with one's religious beliefs.

3. The freedom of religion extends to persons and organizations (churches, denominations, schools, even businesses).

4. Americans do not give up their freedom of religion by participating in the marketplace, partaking of the public square, or interacting with government.

5. Government may not restrict acts or abstentions because of the beliefs they display. ... Except in rare instances, government may not treat the same conduct as lawful when undertaken for secular reasons but unlawful when undertaken for religious reasons. For example, government may not attempt to target religious persons or conduct by allowing the distribution of political leaflets in a park but forbidding the distribution of religious leaflets in the same park.

6. Government may not target religious individuals or entities for special disabilities based on their religion. For instance, government may not exclude religious organizations as such from secular aid programs, at least when the aid is not being used for explicitly religious activities such as worship or proselytization.

7. Government may not target religious individuals or entities through discriminatory enforcement of neutral, generally applicable laws.

8. Government may not officially favor or disfavor particular religious groups.

9. Government may not interfere with the autonomy of a religious organization.

10. Religious employers are entitled to employ only persons whose beliefs and conduct are consistent with the employers' religious precepts.[43]

All over the world, religious freedom is being eroded. Our rights to pray in school, evangelize on the streets, or employ a Christian worker in a Christian workplace are being called into question or in fact denied. This memorandum in the first year of the President's first term underscores his commitment to protecting the religious liberty of Americans, notably American Christians.

PHILIPPIANS 3:18 (ESV)

For many, of whom I have often told you and now tell you even with tears, walk as enemies of the cross of Christ.

EXODUS 5:1 (NAS)

And afterward Moses and Aaron came and said to Pharaoh, "Thus says the LORD, the God of Israel, 'LET MY PEOPLE GO that they may celebrate a feast to Me in the wilderness.'"

October 12, 2017 — President Trump announced the release of two hostages from the Taliban.

THE PRESIDENT: *"In 2012, Caitlan Coleman, an American citizen, and her husband, Joshua Boyle, a Canadian citizen, were taken captive and held hostage by the Haqqani network, a terrorist organization with ties to the Taliban. Ms. Coleman gave birth to the couple's three children while they were in captivity. Yesterday, the United States government, working in conjunction with the Government of Pakistan, secured the release of the Boyle-Coleman family from captivity in Pakistan.*

Today they are free. This is a positive moment for our country's relationship with Pakistan."[44]

PSALM 69:33 (ESV)

For the LORD hears the needy and does not despise his own people who are prisoners.

October 27, 2017 — The Trump Administration motioned to argue on behalf of Jack Phillips, the Colorado Christian baker in the "Gay Wedding Cake Case." Here is a summary of the case:

In 2012, Jack Phillips had refused to bake a wedding cake for a gay couple.

In 2014, the Christian baker was found guilty of discriminating against a same-sex couple by the Colorado Civil Rights Commission.

On December 5, 2017, his case was due to be argued before the US Supreme Court.

The Trump Administration's motion read in part: *"As a general matter, the United States has a substantial interest in the preservation of federal constitutional rights of free expression... In addition, the United States has a particular interest in the scope of such rights in the context of the Colorado statute here, which shares certain features with federal public accommodations laws including Title II of the Civil Rights Act of 1964 and Title III of the Americans with Disabilities Act of 1990."*[45]

In a 7-2 decision on June 4, 2018, the Supreme Court overturned the Colorado Civil Rights Commission's decision, finding it had violated Jack Phillips' right to free exercise of his religion. One decision not to bake a cake had cost Mr. Phillips 6 years of legal battle, a type of harassment that no Christian should ever face in a free nation.

Unfortunately, the battle continues because the liberals did not accept the Supreme Court's decision. The same day that the

Supreme Court ruled in Mr. Phillips' favor, the radical left started an entirely new lawsuit on another basis. They could not allow Phillips' victory to stand. It's part of a campaign of intimidation, to shut up anyone who opposes them. Today Mr. Phillips is back in court.[46]

Healing the pain of legal warfare or "lawfare" waged by the extreme left is the subject of Chapter 6 on "Court Reform" in my book *Trump's Unfinished Business.*[47]

JOHN 16:2-4

2 "...yes, the time is coming that whoever kills you will think that he offers God service.

3 "And these things they will do to you because they have not known the Father nor Me.

4 "But these things I have told you, that when the time comes, you may remember that I told you of them..."

1 PETER 4:14 (ESV)

If you are insulted for the name of Christ, you are blessed, because the Spirit of glory and of God rests upon you.

ACTS 5:29 (ESV)

But Peter and the apostles answered, "We must obey God rather than men."

November 8, 2017 — President Trump proclaimed November 9, 2017, as World Freedom Day, commemorating the fall of the Berlin Wall 28 years earlier.[48] (See the same day in 2019 for more explanation.)

EPHESIANS 2:14 (KJV)

For he is our peace, who hath made both one, and hath broken down the middle wall of partition between us;

November 17, 2017 — President Donald J. Trump proclaimed November 19 through November 25, 2017, as National Family Week.

THE PRESIDENT: *"We cannot take strong families for granted... Federal policy should be directed to facilitating the success of our families. Tax policy is a prime example. My Administration believes that Americans should be able to dedicate more of their resources and earnings to the task and duty of providing for their families... That is why I am committed to cutting taxes for middle-income families—including by expanding the child tax credit—and fundamentally reforming our Nation's outdated tax code."*[49]

JOSHUA 24:15 (ESV)

... But as for me and my house, we will serve the LORD.

1 TIMOTHY 5:8 (ESV)

But if anyone does not provide for his relatives, and especially for members of his household, he has denied the faith and is worse than an unbeliever.

December 6, 2017 — Donald Trump issued a Presidential Proclamation to relocate the US Embassy from Tel Aviv to Jerusalem and to recognize Jerusalem as the Eternal Capital of Israel on the 70th birthday of the nation of Israel.

THE PRESIDENT: *"The foreign policy of the United States is grounded in principled realism, which begins with an honest acknowledgment of plain facts. With respect to the State of Israel, that requires officially recognizing Jerusalem as its capital and relocating the United States Embassy to Israel to Jerusalem as soon as practicable.*

"The Congress, since the Jerusalem Embassy Act of 1995 (Public Law 104-45) (the 'Act'), has urged the United States to recognize Jerusalem as Israel's capital and to relocate our Embassy to Israel to

that city. The United States Senate reaffirmed the Act in a unanimous vote on June 5, 2017.

"Now, 22 years[50] *after the Act's passage, I have determined that it is time for the United States to officially recognize Jerusalem as the capital of Israel. This long overdue recognition of reality is in the best interests of both the United States and the pursuit of peace between Israel and the Palestinians.*

"Seventy years ago, the United States, under President Truman, recognized the State of Israel. Since then, the State of Israel has made its capital in Jerusalem—the capital the Jewish people established in ancient times. Today, Jerusalem is the seat of Israel's government—the home of Israel's parliament, the Knesset; its Supreme Court; the residences of its Prime Minister and President; and the headquarters of many of its government ministries. Jerusalem is where officials of the United States, including the President, meet their Israeli counterparts. It is therefore appropriate for the United States to recognize Jerusalem as Israel's capital."[51]

JOEL 2:1 (NLT)

Sound the trumpet in Jerusalem! Raise the alarm on my holy mountain! Let everyone tremble in fear because the day of the LORD is upon us.

ZEPHANIAH 3:14-15 (ESV)

... Rejoice and exult with all your heart, O daughter of Jerusalem! The Lord has taken away the judgments against you; he has cleared away your enemies...

PSALM 122:6

Pray for the peace of Jerusalem: "May they prosper who love you."

December 8, 2017 — President Trump proclaimed December 10, 2017, as Human Rights Day; December 15, 2017, as

Bill of Rights Day; and the Week Beginning December 10, 2017, as Human Rights Week.

THE PRESIDENT: *"On Bill of Rights Day, we recognize the importance of the first 10 Amendments to our Constitution to protecting our liberty and freedom against the inevitable encroachment of government. Our Founding Fathers understood the threat of expansive, omnipresent government... On June 8, 1789, James Madison, originally skeptical of the need for a bill of rights, introduced in the Congress several amendments to the Constitution that would eventually form the Bill of Rights. During the ensuing debates, Madison told the Congress that because 'all power is subject to abuse' it was worth taking steps to ensure that such abuse 'may be guarded against in a more secure manner.' ... Our God-given, fundamental rights are soon overcome if not safeguarded by the people."*[52]

2 SAMUEL 23:3

The God of Israel said, The Rock of Israel spoke to me: 'He who rules over men must be just, Ruling in the fear of God.'

December 20, 2017 — President Trump commuted the sentence of Sholom Rubashkin.

"Mr. Rubashkin is a 57-year-old father of 10 children. He previously ran the Iowa headquarters of a family business that was the country's largest kosher meat-processing company. In 2009, he was convicted of bank fraud and sentenced thereafter to 27 years in prison. Mr. Rubashkin has now served more than 8 years of that sentence, which many have called excessive in light of its disparity with sentences imposed for similar crimes. This action is not a Presidential pardon."[53]

PROVERBS 31:8 (ESV)

Open your mouth for the mute, for the rights of all who are destitute.

December 20, 2017 — President Trump signed The Tax Cut Act, delivering on his campaign promise.

THE PRESIDENT: "*We're going to cut taxes for the middle class, make the tax code simpler and more fair for everyday Americans, and we are going to bring back the jobs and wealth that have left our country—and most people thought left our country for good.*"[54]

The Tax Cut Act:

- lowered the corporate tax rate from the highest in the developed world of 35 percent to 21 percent—lower than the OECD average;[55]
- nearly doubled the standard deduction of individuals and married couples;
- doubled the Child Tax Credit to $2,000 per child under age 17;
- repealed Obamacare's burdensome individual mandate, which spells relief to households with income below $50,000, or nearly 80 percent of the households that paid the Obamacare mandate penalty in 2016;
- overall provided $5.5 trillion in tax cuts, 60% of which benefited families.

The Bible has provided a template of good government that we ignore at our peril. The Bible commands a flat tax of 10% paid to the Levites or the moral institution of society. This is first, for without God and His laws, there will be rampant theft and corruption in government. The Bible indicates that a state tax of 20% was implemented only for extreme emergencies. Joseph recommended a flat 20% tax rate in Egypt during the 7 years of plenty in preparation for the 7 years of famine.

The normal standard was 10% for religious purposes and 10% for state purposes. This left people with 80% of the fruits of their labor to enjoy, and it left the politicians with a limited budget so they could not embark on military adventurism or reward their friends with lucrative state-subsidized projects, as Obama did for green companies that went bankrupt after receiving $2.2 billion in "clean energy loans"[56] and for website builders that spent $2.1 billion to build a healthcare.gov website that didn't work.[57]

It is unfortunate that so many citizens reject God's ways and rob God's tithe. As a result, they live under man's oppressive ways and keep *less than 50%* of their hard-earned income from work, after all taxes, stamp duties, license fees, registration fees, council rates, VATs and GSTs are accounted for. Singapore comes closest to the Biblical principle of taxing individual income at around 10%. This tiny nation has an honest workforce and one of the strongest economies for a nation its size. God's ways are better and higher than our ways.

MALACHI 3:8-10 (NLT)

8 "Should people cheat God? Yet you have cheated me!

"But you ask, 'What do you mean? When did we ever cheat you?'

"You have cheated me of the tithes and offerings due to me.

9 "You are under a curse, for your whole nation has been cheating me.

10 "Bring all the tithes into the storehouse so there will be enough food in my Temple. If you do," says the LORD of Heaven's Armies, "I will open the windows of heaven for you. I will pour out a blessing so great you won't have enough room to take it in! Try it! Put me to the test!"

December 21, 2017 — President Trump issued an Executive Order "Blocking the Property of Persons Involved in Serious Human Rights Abuse or Corruption."

THE PRESIDENT: "*... the prevalence and severity of human rights abuse and corruption... have reached such scope and gravity that they threaten the stability of international political and economic systems. Human rights abuse and corruption undermine the values that form an essential foundation of stable, secure, and functioning societies...The United States seeks to impose tangible and significant consequences on those who commit serious human rights abuse or engage in corruption, as well as to protect the financial system of the United States from abuse by these same persons. I therefore determine that serious human rights abuse and corruption around the world constitute an unusual and extraordinary threat to the national security, foreign policy, and economy of the United States, and I hereby declare a national emergency to deal with that threat.*

"'I hereby determine and order' the blocking of property owned by 13 named individuals and suspending their entry into the United States."[58]

ISAIAH 1:23 (ESV)

Your princes are rebels and companions of thieves. Everyone loves a bribe and runs after gifts. They do not bring justice to the fatherless, and the widow's cause does not come to them.

December 29, 2017 — President Donald J. Trump proclaimed January 2018 as National Slavery and Human Trafficking Prevention Month.

THE PRESIDENT: *"During National Slavery and Human Trafficking Prevention Month, we recommit ourselves to eradicating the evil of enslavement. Human trafficking is a modern form of the oldest and most barbaric type of exploitation. It has no place in our world. This month we do not simply reflect on this appalling reality. We also pledge to do all in our power to end the horrific practice of human trafficking that plagues innocent victims around the world.*

"Human trafficking is a sickening crime at odds with our very humanity. An estimated ***25 million people*** *are currently victims of human trafficking for both sex and labor.*

"My Administration continues to work to drive out the darkness human traffickers cast upon our world. In February, I signed an Executive Order to dismantle transnational criminal organizations, including those that perpetuate the crime of human trafficking...The Department of State has contributed $25 million to the Global Fund to End Modern Slavery, because of the critical need for cross-nation collaborative action to counter human trafficking... And this month, I will sign into law S. 1536, the Combating Human Trafficking in Commercial Vehicles Act and S. 1532, the No Human Trafficking on Our Roads Act."[59]

PSALM 82:3 (ESV)

Give justice to the weak and the fatherless; maintain the right of the afflicted and the destitute.

CHAPTER 5

SECOND YEAR: 2018

JANUARY 16, 2018 — President Donald J. Trump Proclaims January 16, 2018, as Religious Freedom Day.

THE PRESIDENT: *"Our forefathers, seeking refuge from religious persecution, believed in the eternal truth that freedom is not a gift from the government, but a sacred right from Almighty God. On the coattails of the American Revolution, on January 16, 1786, the Virginia General Assembly passed the Virginia Statute of Religious Freedom. This seminal bill, penned by Thomas Jefferson, states that, 'all men shall be free to profess, and by argument to maintain, their opinions in matters of religion, and that the same shall in no wise diminish, enlarge, or affect their civil capacities.' Five years later, these principles served as the inspiration for the First Amendment, which affirms our right to choose and exercise faith without government coercion or reprisal... The free exercise of religion is a source of personal and national stability, and its preservation is essential to protecting human dignity."*[1]

PSALM 2:2

The kings of the earth set themselves, And the rulers take counsel together, Against the Lord and against His Anointed [Jesus Christ]**...**

January 19, 2018 — President Donald J. Trump proclaimed January 22, 2018, as National Sanctity of Human Life Day.

THE PRESIDENT: "*Much of the greatest suffering in our Nation's history—and, indeed, our planet's history—has been the result of disgracefully misguided attempts to dehumanize whole classes of people based on these immutable characteristics. We cannot let this shameful history repeat itself in new forms, and we must be particularly vigilant to safeguard the most vulnerable lives among us. This is why we observe National Sanctity of Human Life Day: to affirm the truth that all life is sacred, that every person has inherent dignity and worth, and that no class of people should ever be discarded as "non-human.*

"Reverence for every human life, one of the values for which our Founding Fathers fought, defines the character of our Nation... Science continues to support and build the case for life. Medical technologies allow us to see images of the unborn children moving their newly formed fingers and toes, yawning, and even smiling. Those images present us with irrefutable evidence that babies are growing within their mothers' wombs—precious, unique lives, each deserving a future filled with promise and hope. We can also now operate on babies in utero to stave off life-threatening diseases. These important medical advances give us an even greater appreciation for the humanity of the unborn...Thankfully, the number of abortions, which has been in steady decline since 1980, is now at a historic low. Though the fight to protect life is not yet over, we commit to advocating each day for all who cannot speak for themselves."[2]

January 28, 2018 — President Trump became the second sitting President to address the World Economic Forum Annual Meeting, aka Davos.

This was the President's greatest anti-globalist speech of his first term. It set a tone that no globalist power-monger could doubt again. Unlike the elites at Davos, President Trump defended the Biblical concept of sovereign nations and opposed the demonic rise of an ancient hubris called the Tower of Babel.

Note carefully that President Trump distinguished between two kinds of globalism: **economic globalism** vs. **political globalism.** One is voluntary international trade (which he considers good for all); the other is coercive central control (which he considers detrimental to Americans).

THE PRESIDENT: *"I am here to deliver a simple message: There has never been a better time to hire, to build, to invest, and to grow in the United States. AMERICA IS OPEN FOR BUSINESS AND WE ARE COMPETITIVE ONCE AGAIN.*

"The American economy is by far the largest in the world and we've just enacted the most significant tax cuts and reform IN AMERICAN HISTORY.

"We massively cut taxes for the middle class and small businesses to let working families keep more of their hard-earned money.

"We lowered our corporate tax rate from 35 percent, all the way down to 21 percent. As a result, millions of workers have received tax cut bonuses from their employers in amounts as large as three thousand dollars...

"Now is the perfect time to bring your business, your jobs, and your investments to the United States of America.

"This is especially true because we have undertaken the most extensive regulatory reduction ever conceived. Regulation is stealth taxation.

"In the United States, like in many countries, ***unelected bureaucrats have imposed crushing anti-business and anti-worker regulations on our citizens with no vote, no legislative debate, and no real accountability.***

"In America, those days are OVER.

"I pledged to eliminate two unnecessary regulations for every one new regulation. We have succeeded beyond our highest expectations. Instead of two-for-one, we have cut TWENTY-TWO burdensome regulations for every ONE new rule.

"... I believe in America. As President of the United States, I will always put America First. Just like the leaders of other countries should put their countries first.

"But America First does not mean America alone. *When the United States grows, so does the world...*

"We cannot have free and open trade if some countries exploit the system at the expense of others. We support free trade, but it needs to be FAIR and RECIPROCAL.

"... The United States will no longer turn a blind eye to unfair economic practices, including ***massive intellectual property theft, industrial subsidies, and pervasive state-led economic planning.*** *These and other predatory behaviors are distorting global markets and harming businesses and workers—not just in the United States, but around the globe."*[3]

Invited to share in the European elites' globalist pie, President Trump symbolically threw the pie in their faces. They could not miss his intent. Their game was up. He was calling them out.

2 PETER 2:19 (ESV)

They promise them freedom, but they themselves are slaves of corruption...

Trump exposed their duplicity. They have been deceiving the public by using the word "globalism" to mean two opposite things—a linguistic trickery called "equivocation."

On the one hand, globalism means "voluntary international trade of goods and services." This is universally desirable. It's how we get our amazing tech gadgets, clothes and foods from all around the world. Everybody wants that! Trump affirmed, "America is open for business" or for this type of global commerce.

On the other hand, the same word globalism is used to mean "coercive control of people, habits, movements, and taxes." It speaks of arbitrary rules made by unelected officials. It includes global financial credit scores, surveillance by drones, mass quarantines, draconian lockdowns.

Who wants this? The globalists do. The people whom they have brainwashed do.

Who doesn't want it? We the People

...and Donald J. Trump.

THE PRESIDENT continues his address to the globalists at Davos: *"Just like we expect the leaders of other countries to protect their interests, as President of the United States, I will always protect the interests of our country, our companies, and our workers...*

"From my first international G-7 summit, to the G-20, to the U.N. General Assembly, to APEC, to the World Trade Organization, and today at the World Economic Forum, my administration has not only been present, but has driven our message that ***we are all stronger when free and sovereign Nations cooperate*** *toward shared goals—and shared dreams."*[4]

Such defense of the people's rights to autonomy is the real reason the Establishment hates him, wants to remove him, and may even want to kill him.

Christians should pray for Trump because his greatest achievement may be protecting America from a globalist takeover that will usher in the Biblical Anti-Christ.

REVELATION 17:13 (ESV)

These are of one mind, and they hand over their power and authority to the beast.

The "Beast" is a code for the person of the Anti-Christ and/or the system of Anti-Christ. This system will not allow you to "buy or sell," go to restaurants or travel, unless you accept a mark, a name, or a number on your hand or on your forehead.

REVELATION 13:16-17

He causes all, both small and great, rich and poor, free and slave, to receive a mark on their right hand or on their foreheads, and that no one may BUY OR SELL except one who has the MARK or the NAME of the beast, or the NUMBER of his name.

February 21, 2018 — President Trump issued a Proclamation on the Death of Billy Graham.

THE PRESIDENT: *"As a mark of respect for the memory of Reverend Billy Graham, I hereby order, by the authority vested in me by the Constitution and the laws of the United States of America, that on the day of his interment, the flag of the United States shall be flown at half-staff at the White House and upon all public buildings and grounds, at all military posts and naval stations, and on all naval vessels of the Federal Government in the District of Columbia and throughout the United States and its Territories and possessions until sunset on such day. I also direct that the flag shall be flown at half-staff for the same period at all United States embassies, legations, consular offices, and other facilities abroad, including all military facilities and naval vessels and stations."*[5]

ISAIAH 28:5

He will swallow up death forever, And the Lord God will wipe away tears from all faces...

March 23, 2018 — The Trump Administration and the Department of Defense (DOD) issued a new policy on homosexuals and transgenders serving in the military.

As reported by the Family Research Council, Trump's policy allows "existing personnel to remain in the military while preventing those who have been diagnosed with 'gender dysphoria' or had undergone gender transition surgery from joining the military. Those who are transgender and stable for

36 months could join so long as they serve in accordance with their biological sex."[6]

> **MATTHEW 19:4**
> **And He** [Jesus] **answered and said to them** [the Pharisees], **"Have you not read that He who made them at the beginning 'made them male and female,'"**

March 29, 2018 — President Trump proclaimed April 2018 as National Child Abuse Prevention Month.

THE PRESIDENT: *"National Child Abuse Prevention Month is an annual reminder that not every home is a haven of acceptance and unconditional love. Too often, childhood is marred with pain, violence, neglect, and abuse, which can have lifelong psychological, emotional, and physical consequences. At no fault of their own, some children are subjected to the most depraved forms of child abuse and neglect, without reprieve and, sometimes, without any knowledge that they are being maltreated. The statistics are shocking: a quarter of all children experience some form of child abuse or neglect in their lifetime. The financial consequences of this depravity are dire. By some estimates, the lifetime cost of child abuse and neglect is $124 billion per year. The human cost—measured in lost development, potential, and flourishing—is incalculable.*

"To improve the statistics and the well-being of our Nation's children, we must become more aware of the signs and symptoms of child abuse and take action as necessary...The Child Welfare Information Gateway (CWIG) notes that children who show sudden changes in behavior, who have not received treatment for physical or medical problems brought to their parents' attention, or who are always watchful, as if preparing for something bad to happen, may be exhibiting signs of child abuse.

"We must always remember that all children are blessings from our Creator... They are a source of unmatched joy, and they represent our Nation's future. It is thus our civic and moral

responsibility to help every child experience a childhood free from abuse and mistreatment, guiding them toward a future full of hope and promise."[7]

MARK 9:42 (NIV)

If anyone causes one of these little ones—those who believe in me—to stumble, it would be better for them if a large millstone were hung around their neck and they were thrown into the sea.

April 11, 2018 — President Trump proclaimed April 12 through April 19, 2018, as the Days of Remembrance of Victims of the Holocaust.

THE PRESIDENT: *"The Holocaust, known in Hebrew as 'Shoah,' was the culmination of the Nazi regime's 'Final Solution to the Jewish Question,' an attempt to eradicate the Jewish population in Europe. Although spearheaded by one individual, this undertaking could not have happened without the participation of many others who recruited, persuaded, and coerced in their efforts to incite the worst of human nature and carry out the ugliest of depravity. The abject brutality of the Nazi regime, coupled with the failure of Western leaders to confront the Nazis early on, created an environment that encouraged and enflamed anti-Semitic sentiment and drove people to engage in depraved, dehumanizing conduct.*

"By the end, the Nazis and their conspirators had murdered 6 million men, women, and children, simply because they were Jews...

"We have a responsibility to convey the lessons of the Holocaust to future generations, and together as Americans, we have a moral obligation to combat antisemitism, confront hate, and prevent genocide. We must ensure that the history of the Holocaust remains forever relevant and that no people suffer these tragedies ever again."[8]

ISAIAH 62:4 (GNT)

No longer will you be called "Forsaken," Or your land be called "The Deserted Wife." Your new name will be "God Is Pleased with Her." Your land will be called "Happily Married," Because the LORD is pleased with you And will be like a husband to your land.

April 26, 2018 — President Trump's choice for Secretary of State, Mike Pompeo, was confirmed by the Senate. Secretary Pompeo is a Christian who was instrumental in negotiating the release of Christians out of North Korea and Turkey. He would later give a defining speech on "Being a Christian Leader" at the Gaylord Opryland Hotel:

"... when I started my time at the United States Military Academy, there were two young men...who invited me to a Bible study. They were very intentional to me in explaining God's Word. And after some study and discipleship with them, they helped me begin my walk with Christ.

"... I keep a Bible open on my desk, and I try every morning to try and get in a little bit of time with the Book. I need my mind renewed with truth each day. And part of that truth is, as my son reminds me, is to be humble. Proverbs says, 'With the humble is wisdom.'

"... the Book of James [says]: 'Everyone should be quick to listen, and slow to speak.'... Every day... I engage with foreign leaders who sit across the table from me, or sit in a room, and I try to understand what it is they want... sound relationships absolutely depend on open ears. Good listening means more than just hearing; it means not rushing to judgment before you hear every side of a particular fact set. This comes through so clearly in Proverbs, which say, 'The one who states his case first seems right, until the other comes and examines him.'"[9]

It must not be easy for Mike Pompeo to be Secretary of State and live out his Christian convictions. The balance seems to be that he applies his faith to himself, but does not hesitate to apply the power of the United States on others, which reminds me of this Scripture.

ROMANS 13:4 (ESV)

For he is God's servant for your good. But if you do wrong, be afraid, for he does not bear the sword in vain. For he is the servant of God, an avenger who carries out God's wrath on the wrongdoer.

April 30, 2018 — President Trump defended persecuted Christians as he met with the President of Nigeria at the Oval Office.

THE PRESIDENT: *"Nigeria is the largest democracy in Africa. As I conveyed to President Buhari in our discussions, the United States deeply values and appreciates Nigeria's role as a strong, democratic leader in the region...*

"Nigeria is also leading African nations in the fight against Boko Haram, and— another ruthless jihadist terrorist group. You've been reading about them. They kidnapped the young girls and young women, many of whom never are seen again. It's tough stuff. This summer, it was my honor to meet with two brave young women, Joy Bishara and Lydia Pogu, who were kidnapped by Boko Haram in April of 2014 at the secondary school in Nigeria. I was deeply moved by their inspiring stories...

"I told Joy and Lydia, my administration is committed to combatting both jihadist terrorism and the scourge of human trafficking and smuggling. In the world today, there is more human trafficking than there has ever been—if you can believe this. They use the Internet better than almost anybody is able to use the Internet. So think of it, in a modern world, in this world, there's more human trafficking and slavery than at any time in the history of this world. It's hard to believe...

"Finally, we're deeply concerned by religious violence in Nigeria, including the burning of churches, and the killing and persecution of

Christians. It's a horrible story. We encourage Nigeria and the federal, state, and local leaders to do everything in their power to immediately secure the affected communities and to protect innocent civilians of all faiths, including Muslims and including Christians."[10]

The killing of Christians has been an issue largely ignored by Western political leaders. President Trump was courageous to defend Christians internationally.

JOHN 16:2 (NLT)

...the time is coming when those who kill you will think they are doing a holy service for God.

May 3, 2018 — President Trump proclaimed May 3 as a National Day of Prayer.

THE PRESIDENT: *"Prayer has been a source of guidance, strength, and wisdom since the founding of our Republic. When the Continental Congress gathered in Philadelphia to contemplate freedom from Great Britain, the delegates prayed daily for guidance. Their efforts produced the Declaration of Independence and its enumeration of the self-evident truths that we all cherish today...*

"In 1988, the Congress, by Public Law 100-307, as amended, called on the President to issue each year a proclamation designating the first Thursday in May as a National Day of Prayer, 'on which the people of the United States may turn to God in prayer and meditation at churches, in groups, and as individuals.'"[11]

2 CHRONICLES 7:14

if My people who are called by My name will humble themselves, and pray and seek My face, and turn from their wicked ways, then I will hear from heaven, and will forgive their sin and heal their land.

May 8, 2018 — President Trump announced US withdrawal from Obama's Iran Nuclear Deal.

The deal was poorly negotiated and flawed on many levels. Obama gave Iran $400 million in unmarked cash delivered on the same day Iran released US prisoners (January 17, 2016). Obama gave Iran an additional $1.3 billion paid over the next 19 days and unfroze $150 billion worth of Iranian assets, which analysts suspect helped underwrite Iran's military interference in Syria, Yemen, Iraq, and elsewhere.[12]

What did the US get in return?

A promise that Iran would not develop nuclear weapons. A promise which the Bible already predicts will be broken in Ezekiel 38. A promise which remains virtually unenforceable due to the weak inspection and verification program and an automatic sunset clause. This does not mean the Iranian people are enemies. On the contrary, we believe Iran was the home of Queen Esther and the Prophet Daniel, and has had a rich history worth preserving. Obama's deal did not help the Iranian people gain freedom from an oppressive regime but strengthened it. It also failed to restrict Iran's ballistic missile program. No wonder Trump called it "the worst deal ever."

In his memorandum, the President stated: *"Since its inception in 1979 as a revolutionary theocracy, the Islamic Republic of Iran has declared its hostility to the United States and its allies and partners. Iran remains the world's leading state sponsor of terrorism, and provides assistance to Hezbollah, Hamas, the Taliban, al-Qa'ida, and other terrorist networks. Iran also continues to fuel sectarian violence in Iraq and support vicious civil wars in Yemen and Syria. It commits grievous human rights abuses, and arbitrarily detains foreigners, including United States citizens, on spurious charges without due process of law.*

"... The preceding administration [Obama] attempted to meet the threat of Iran's pursuit of nuclear capabilities through United States participation in the Joint Comprehensive Plan of Action (JCPOA) on Iran's nuclear program. The JCPOA lifted nuclear-related sanctions on Iran and provided it with other significant benefits in exchange for

its temporary commitments to constrain its uranium enrichment program and to not conduct work related to nuclear fuel reprocessing, the two critical pathways to acquiring weapons-grade nuclear material. Some believed the JCPOA would moderate Iran's behavior.

"Since the JCPOA's inception, however, Iran has only escalated its destabilizing activities in the surrounding region. Iranian or Iran-backed forces have gone on the march in Syria, Iraq, and Yemen, and continue to control parts of Lebanon and Gaza. Meanwhile, Iran has publicly declared it would deny the International Atomic Energy Agency (IAEA) access to military sites...

"Iran's behavior threatens the national interest of the United States... It is the policy of the United States that Iran be denied a nuclear weapon and intercontinental ballistic missiles; that Iran's network and campaign of regional aggression be neutralized... The Secretary of State and the Secretary of the Treasury shall immediately begin taking steps to re-impose all United States sanctions lifted or waived in connection with the JCPOA...."[13]

EZEKIEL 38:5 (NLT)

Persia, Ethiopia, and Libya will join you, too, with all their weapons.

Biblical Persia, Ethiopia, and Libya are now modern Islamic Iran, Islamic Sudan, and Islamic Libya in prophecy. All three will take part in a Turkish-led invasion of Israel, known as the **Gog-Magog War**. The weapons deployed will be radioactive, as described in Zechariah 14:12 and Ezekiel 39. After the war, prophecy details a cleanup process that is completely alien to any description of ancient post-combat cleanup. And it will last more than seven months. It seems that due to the radioactivity left in the combat zone, a Hazmat[14] team will be sent to find bones, mark them, and then a burial team will bury them in a special containment zone.

ZECHARIAH 14:12 (NLT)

12 And the Lord will send a plague on all the nations that fought against Jerusalem. Their people will become like walking corpses, their flesh rotting away. Their eyes will rot in their sockets, and their tongues will rot in their mouths.

No weapon in the ancient world could fulfill this devastating description. But photographs of the after-effects of the atomic bombing of Hiroshima showed Japanese people disintegrated right where they stood, leaving only a shadow on the pavements. This 2,000-year-old verse seems prophetic of our modern nuclear weapons being used in the Middle East.

EZEKIEL 39:12-16 (NLT)

12 It will take seven months for the people of Israel to bury the bodies and cleanse the land.

13 "Everyone in Israel will help, for it will be a glorious victory for Israel when I demonstrate my glory on that day," says the Sovereign LORD.

14 After seven months, teams of men will be appointed to search the land for skeletons to bury, so the land will be made clean again.

15 Whenever bones are found, a marker will be set up so the burial crews will take them to be buried in the Valley of Gog's Hordes.

16 (There will be a town there named Hamonah, which means "horde.") And so the land will finally be cleansed.

The fact that Obama did so much to enable Islamic terrorists abroad, while refusing to defend traditional marriage at home, earned him the title of "America's Most Biblically-Hostile US President" by Christian historian David Barton.[15]

May 9, 2018 — Trump announced that he and Secretary of

State Mike Pompeo had negotiated the release of Three Americans, Pastor Kim Dong Chul, Tony Kim and Kim Hak Song from Detainment in North Korea. They arrived home on US soil the next day.[16]

THE VICE PRESIDENT: "*Thanks to President Trump's tough-minded diplomacy, three Americans held hostage in North Korea are coming home. While our administration is encouraged that North Korea freed these innocent hostages, we will not let off the pressure until we achieve full denuclearization. Our Secretary of State Mike Pompeo did a remarkable job overseeing the release of Kim Dong Chul, Tony Kim, and Kim Hak Song –and to them I say: safe travels and welcome home.*"[17]

May 10, 2018 — President Trump received bipartisan praise for the release of three American hostages on American soil.

Harry Kazianis, Senior Director of Korean Studies at the Center for the National Interest: "*President Trump deserves high praise... not only for securing the release of the three US citizens, but also for prompting Kim Jong Un to hold talks with South Korean President Moon Jae-in recently, and for setting up a Trump-Kim summit in the near future. These steps have hopefully averted what could have been a nuclear war.*"[18]

Senate Majority Leader Mitch McConnell (R-KY): "*This morning the world has learned that Secretary of State Mike Pompeo is on his way back from North Korea with three American prisoners after securing their release. Two were detained last year, one had been in captivity since 2015, and now following successful discussions, all three are on their way back to the US with our secretary of state.*"[19]

MATTHEW 25:36-40

"I was naked and you clothed Me; I was sick and you visited Me; I was in prison and you came to Me." Then the righteous will answer Him, saying, "Lord...when did we see You sick, or in prison, and come to You?" And the King will

answer and say to them, "Assuredly, I say to you, inasmuch as you did it to one of the least of these My brethren, you did it to Me."

May 14, 2018 — The US Embassy officially relocated from Tel Aviv to Jerusalem. The event was timed to coincide with the 70th anniversary of Israel's Declaration of Independence.

ISAIAH 65:18

But be glad and rejoice forever in what I create; For behold, I create Jerusalem as a rejoicing, And her people a joy.

May 24, 2018 — President Trump made an "Executive Act of Clemency Posthumously to John Arthur 'Jack' Johnson."

THE PRESIDENT: *"Born in 1878 in Galveston, Texas, to former slaves, Johnson overcame difficult circumstances to reach the heights of the boxing world and inspired generations with his tenacity and independent spirit...*

"Congress has supported numerous resolutions calling for Johnson's pardon. These resolutions enjoyed widespread bipartisan support, including from the Congressional Black Caucus...

"In light of these facts and in recognition of his historic athletic achievements and contributions to society, the President believes Jack Johnson is worthy of a posthumous pardon. President Trump is taking this unusual step to 'right a wrong' that occurred in our history and honor the legacy of a champion."[20]

1 SAMUEL 31:12-13

all the valiant men arose and traveled all night, and took the body of Saul and the bodies of his sons from the wall of Beth Shan...Then they took their bones and buried them under the tamarisk tree at Jabesh...

Honoring the dead is a characteristic of godly people. David honored Saul when he died, even though he was cruel to David when he was alive. David said of him and his son Jonathan, "How the mighty have fallen." (2 Samuel 1:25) There is honor and decorum due to the dead.

Even though the spirit is the only eternal part of our being, the body is holy because it houses the spirit, and it will one day be raised in the resurrection.[21] Honoring the dead and giving their bodies a proper burial is a New Testament concept.

HEBREWS 11:22

By faith Joseph, when he was dying, made mention of the departure of the children of Israel, and gave instructions concerning his bones.

May 25, 2018 — President Donald J. Trump proclaimed Memorial Day, May 28, 2018, as a Day of Prayer for Permanent Peace.

Author's personal note: This is the day I was saved from sin by Jesus Christ, so I am interested in what this day represents to others in the world. I long very much for permanent peace, peace from injustice, peace between enemies, peace between sinful men and a holy God. It is significant to me that this proclaimed "day of peace" came with a price—the sacrifice of men who confronted evil and won the victory of war against tyrants.

THE PRESIDENT: *"On Memorial Day, we pause in solemn gratitude to pay tribute to the brave patriots who laid down their lives defending peace and freedom while in military service to our great Nation... Our 151 national cemeteries serve as the final resting place for millions of people, including veterans from every war and conflict, many of whom died while serving our country. We remain duty-bound to honor those who made the ultimate sacrifice on our behalf and to remember them with thankfulness...The sacrifices of our hallowed dead demand our Nation's highest honor and deepest gratitude. On this day, let us also unite in prayer for lasting peace in our troubled world so that future generations will enjoy the blessings of liberty and independence."*[22]

EPHESIANS 2:13-14

But now in Christ Jesus you who once were far off have been brought near by the blood of Christ. For he himself is our peace...

Peace is not cheap. Our eternal peace cost the blood of the sinless Son of God.

May 26, 2018 — Trump announced the release of an American couple Josh and Thamy Holt from Venezuela. They had spent 21 months in a prison inmates call "hell on earth." When they arrived on US soil, they were invited to meet the President at the Oval Office. After spending two days in medical care, they were released to return to their home state of Utah on May 28.

From the Oval Office, President Trump stated, "We've had 17 prisoners released during the Trump administration. Most people don't know that."[23] This number will triple by the end of his first term.

May 31, 2018 — President Trump issued an Executive Grant of Clemency (Full Pardon) to Dinesh D'Souza, an Indian-born Christian conservative who acted as a policy advisor to Ronald Reagan from 1987 to 1988. In 2012, D'Souza released an anti-Obama documentary titled *2016: Obama's America*. It earned $33 million, making it the highest-grossing conservative documentary of all time.[24] D'Souza claimed the Obama Administration then targeted him for illegal campaign contribution.

THE PRESS SECRETARY: "Mr. D'Souza was, in the President's opinion, a victim of selective prosecution for violations of campaign finance laws. Mr. D'Souza accepted responsibility for his actions, and also completed community service by teaching English to citizens and immigrants seeking citizenship.

In light of these facts, the President has determined that Mr. D'Souza is fully worthy of this pardon."[25]

This pardon qualified as a pro-Christian accomplishment because it defended not only free speech, but also a Christian scholar. D'Souza is an author of Christian apologetics, including *What's So Great About Christianity?* (2007). He served as president of The King's College, a Christian school in New York City, from 2010 to 2012. His wife, Dixie, is an evangelical. In an interview with *Christianity Today*, D'Souza explained that although he was raised Catholic, he now identifies as a nondenominational Christian:

"I'm quite happy to acknowledge my Catholic background; at the same time, I'm very comfortable with Reformation theology. I'm comfortable with the evangelical world...

"I do not describe myself as Catholic today. But I don't want to renounce it either...I say I have a Catholic origin or background. I say I'm a nondenominational Christian, and I'm comfortable with born-again.

"Christians spend a lot of time in intramural type debates and squabbles: Are you a Catholic or Protestant; if you are Protestant, what type are you; are you pre-millennial or post-millennial; what position do you take on Genesis 1? I would comfortably describe myself as a born-again Christian..."[26]

MATTHEW 5:11-13

11 Blessed are you when they revile and persecute you, and say all kinds of evil against you falsely for My sake.

12 Rejoice and be exceedingly glad, for great is your reward in heaven, for so they persecuted the prophets who were before you.

13 "You are the salt of the earth...

June 6, 2018 — One week after meeting Kim Kardashian and Jared Kushner, who both sought clemency for Alice Marie Johnson, President Donald Trump commuted her life sentence. She had served 21 years of a life sentence without parole for a first-time, non-violent drug offense. Her application for a second chance was denied by President Obama.

WHITE HOUSE STATEMENT: *"Today, President Donald J. Trump granted a commutation to Alice Marie Johnson, a 63-year-old great-grandmother who has served almost 22 years in Federal prison for a first-time criminal offense.*

"Ms. Johnson has accepted responsibility for her past behavior and has been a model prisoner over the past two decades. Despite receiving a life sentence, Alice worked hard to rehabilitate herself in prison, and act as a mentor to her fellow inmates...

"While this Administration will always be very tough on crime, it believes that those who have paid their debt to society and worked hard to better themselves while in prison deserve a second chance."[27]

It is important to note that this commutation was not a mere token. Within 6 months, President Trump would sign into law a historic piece of legislation on criminal reform known as The First Step Act. Ms. Johnson would be a guest of the President at his State of the Union Address on February 5, 2019, and his guest at his acceptance speech for the Republican Party's Presidential nomination on August 27, 2020. He would give her a full pardon the next day based on her exemplary life in prison and for her "incredible job since she's been out."[28]

1 PETER 4:14-16

14 If you are reproached for the name of Christ, blessed are you, for the Spirit of glory and of God rests upon you. On their part He is blasphemed, but on your part He is glorified.

15 But let none of you suffer as a murderer, a thief, an evildoer, or as a busybody in other people's matters.

16 Yet if anyone suffers as a Christian, let him not be ashamed, but let him glorify God in this matter.

July 9, 2018 — President Donald J. Trump announced his intent to nominate Judge Brett Kavanaugh to the Supreme Court of the United States.

THE WHITE HOUSE: *"The nomination of Judge Kavanaugh comes after a selection process marked by an historic degree of transparency, including the President's public disclosure of a list of 25 highly qualified potential nominees to the Supreme Court.*

"Judge Kavanaugh has served as a judge on the US Court of Appeals for the District of Columbia Circuit since 2006, authoring more than 300 opinions, including 11 that have been affirmed by the Supreme Court. Before becoming a judge, he served in the George W. Bush administration, first as an Associate Counsel and then Senior Associate Counsel, and subsequently as Assistant to the President and Staff Secretary...

"Judge Kavanaugh has earned a reputation as a brilliant jurist with impeccable legal credentials, and he is universally respected for his intellect, as well as his ability to persuade and build consensus. Judge Kavanaugh lives in Maryland with his wife Ashley and their two daughters."[29]

ACTS 6:3

Therefore, brethren, select from among you seven men of good reputation, full of the Spirit and of wisdom, whom we may put in charge of this task.

PROVERBS 16:10 (NLT)

The king speaks with divine wisdom; he must never judge unfairly.

July 26, 2018 — The first Ministerial to Advance Religious Freedom was hosted by Secretary of State Mike Pompeo, at the direction of the President, and held at the Harry S. Truman Building. The event brought together representatives of 80 nations, including survivors of religious persecution.

THE VICE PRESIDENT: "*...after this great nation secured our independence, the American Founders enshrined religious freedom as the first freedom in the Constitution of the United States...religious freedom is in the interest of the peace and security of the world. Those nations that reject religious freedom breed radicalism and resentment in their citizens...a stunning 83 percent of the world's population live in nations where religious freedom is either threatened or even banned...The list of religious freedom violators is long; their crimes and oppressions span the width of our world. Here in our own hemisphere, in Nicaragua, the government of Daniel Ortega is virtually waging war on the Catholic Church...religious persecution is growing in both scope and scale in the world's most populous country, the People's Republic of China. The State Department's annual International Religious Freedom report has labeled China as a religious freedom violator every year since 1999... But for all of China's abuses, their neighbor in North Korea is much worse...Today, as we gather at this ministerial, an estimated 130,000 North Koreans are imprisoned for life in unimaginably brutal slave labor camps. Contrasted with a thriving Christian community in South Korea...today, I'm also pleased, as Vice President, to announce that the United States will launch the new International Religious Freedom Fund.*"[30]

June 12, 2018 — The historic Singapore Summit was the first time the President of the United States met with the leader of North Korea. It was a masterful, carefully choreographed example of *Art of the Deal* negotiation.

Singapore was no doubt selected by President Trump to showcase to Kim the success of an Asian nation that cooperates with the world community. Singapore is an impressive city state that boasts efficient transport, clean streets, low crime, modern facilities, and beautiful gardens. It's a combination that's the envy of any nation.

During the meeting, President Trump showed Kim a 4-minute video that was made like an action movie trailer. It appealed to Kim's youth, to his pride, and to his sense of historic standing. All this was achieved without paying him millions of dollars. In other words, no politician could have done it.

It took a businessman like Donald Trump to come to a political summit with a promo presentation that's typical of a business meeting. Trump showed Kim through the location they were in and by the video they were watching that North Korea could have an economic boom if it stopped testing nuclear weapons.

Let me highlight some of the content in this effective video.

Narrator: "...the light of prosperity and innovation has burned bright for most of the world (picture of Singapore)... there comes a time when only a few are called upon to make a difference (photo of Chairman Kim first, then President Trump) ...the past (photo of a North Korean soldier standing the demilitarized zone) doesn't have to be the future (happy Korean children)...Destiny Pictures presents a story of opportunity...of two men, two leaders, one destiny...(basketball, Singapore)..."

At 2:39 seconds, the normally darkened map of North Korea at night explodes with light.

Narrator: "A new world can begin today, one of friendship, respect (photo of President Trump and Sylvester Stallone), and good will. Be part of that world, where the doors of opportunity are ready to be opened—investments from around the world, where you can have medical breakthroughs, an abundance of resources, innovative technology, new discoveries. What if? Can history be changed? (photo of Kim)...

And when can this moment in history begin? It comes

down to a choice....the world will be watching, anticipating, hoping. Will this leader choose to advance his country and be part of a new world—be the hero of his people? **Will he shake the hand of peace and enjoy prosperity like he has never seen?** A great life? Or more isolation? Which path will be chosen? Featuring president Donald Trump and Chairman Kim Jong Un in a meeting to remake history, to shine in the sun. One moment. One choice. What if? The future remains to be written."[31]

The outcome of this meeting was signed a joint statement, agreeing to new peaceful relations, the denuclearization of the Korean Peninsula, recovery of soldiers' remains, and follow-up negotiations between high-level officials.[32]

As a sign of goodwill, President Trump announced after the Singapore Summit that the US military would discontinue "provocative" joint military exercises with South Korea, something Trump would have liked to do anyway.

He gave the North Korean leader what he wanted—a sense of importance on world stage. In return he got deescalation of tension, military muscle-flexing, bomb testing, missile launching, and the bodies of American MIAs returned to their families. No other president could have conceived of this strategy and executed it so efficiently. The cost to America was very low. The benefit to the world was disproportionally great. When Obama left the Oval Office, he was sure that the next war would be waged with North Korea.[33] Instead, for 4 years the world had respite from the threat of North Korea and South Korea's biggest threat was its own coronavirus problem in 2020.

MATTHEW 5:9

Blessed are the peacemakers, For they shall be called sons of God.

July 29, 2018 — President Trump commuted the sentence of Ted Suhl.

THE WHITE HOUSE: *"Mr. Suhl ran faith-based behavioral healthcare treatment centers for juveniles in Arkansas. Investigators alleged that Mr. Suhl participated in a bribery scheme to increase Medicaid payments to his company. Federal prosecutors in Arkansas declined to pursue the case, but prosecutors in Washington decided to move forward with the prosecution. Although acquitted on half of the charges filed against him, he was sentenced to seven years in prison.*

"Mr. Suhl was a pillar of his community before his prosecution and a generous contributor to several charities. He has been a model prisoner while serving his sentence, maintaining a spotless disciplinary record. Mr. Suhl's request for clemency is strongly supported by former Arkansas Governor Mike Huckabee and former United States Attorney Bud Cummins of the Eastern District of Arkansas, each of whom have devoted considerable time and effort to securing his release."[34]

LUKE 4:18 (NIV)

"The Spirit of the Lord is on me, because he has anointed me to proclaim good news to the poor. He has sent me to proclaim freedom for the prisoners and recovery of sight for the blind, to set the oppressed free,

August 1, 2018 — President Trump relied on Executive Order 13818 to sanction two Turkish officials over the detention of American pastor Andrew Brunson. The Administration also put tariffs on Turkey, which contributed to the crash of its currency, the lira. Turkish President Erdogan called these US actions "economic war" against Turkey.[35] These actions led to the eventual release of Pastor Brunson in October 2018.

PROVERBS 21:15 (ESV)

When justice is done, it is a joy to the righteous but terror to evildoers.

August 1, 2018 — President Trump invited inner-city pastors to make their voices heard at the Cabinet Room. Among the leaders were Pastor Paula White, Dr. Alveda King (niece of Dr. Martin Luther King Jr.), and African American Pastor Darrell Scott.

PASTOR DARRELL SCOTT: "*... people ask me why do I defend him so vociferously. And I say it's easy for me to do it because I know him, and he's shown me his heart, and I know he has a heart for all Americans.*

"*And I will say this: This administration has taken a lot of people by surprise. And it's going to surprise you guys even more, because this is probably the most proactive administration regarding urban America and the faith-based community in my lifetime. And I'll be 60 years old in December.*

"*... to be honest, this is probably going to be... the most pro-black President that we've had in our lifetime because... this President actually wants to prove something to our community, our faith-based community and our ethnic community.*

"*The last President didn't feel like he had to. He felt like he didn't have to prove it. He got a pass. This President is—this administration is probably going to be more proactive regarding urban revitalization and prison reform than any President in your lifetime.*

"*If we work together, give him a chance. Don't pay any attention to these guys back here (Referring to the media. Laughs.).*"[36]

ISAIAH 51:7 (ESV)

"Listen to me, you who know righteousness, the people in whose heart is my law; fear not the reproach of man, nor be dismayed at their revilings.

August 20, 2018 — The last known Nazi collaborator living on American soil was deported by the direct order of President Trump. The 95-year-old man, Jakiw Palij, was an armed guard in a brutal Nazi prison camp who came to America in 1949. His citizenship was revoked in 2003 and a judge ordered him to be deported in 2005, but no country would take him.[37] Trump finished the job and deported Palij to Germany, sending a strong message that America will never tolerate anti-Semitism again.

LUKE 12:2 (ESV)

Nothing is covered up that will not be revealed, or hidden that will not be known.

GENESIS 12:3

I will bless those who bless you, And I will curse him who curses you...

August 27, 2018 — President Trump made remarks at a dinner with Evangelical Leaders.

THE PRESIDENT: *"In the last 18 months alone, we have stopped the Johnson Amendment from interfering with your First Amendment rights.*[38] *(Applause.) A big deal. It's a big deal.*

"We've taken action to defend the religious conscience of doctors, nurses, teachers, students, preachers, faith groups, and religious employers.

"We sent the entire executive branch guidance on protecting religious liberty. Big deal. Brought the Faith and Opportunity Initiative to the White House.

"Reinstated the Mexico City Policy we first put into place. And if you know, if you study it--and most of you know about this--first under President Ronald Reagan, not since then—the Mexico City Policy. (Applause.)

"We proposed regulations to prevent Title 10 taxpayer funding

from subsidizing abortion. I was the first President to stand in the Rose Garden to address the March for Life. First one. (Applause.)

"My administration has strongly spoken out against religious persecution around the world, including the persecution of Christians. All over the world, what's going on. (Applause.) And for that, we've become not only a strong voice but a very, very powerful force. We're stopping a lot of bad things from happening.

"We brought home hostages from North Korea, including an American pastor. And we're fighting to release Pastor Brunson from Turkey. (Applause.)

"...We've recognized the capital of Israel and opened the US Embassy in Jerusalem. (Applause.)

"... Every day, we're standing for religious believers, because we know that faith and family, not government and bureaucracy, are the center of American life. (Applause.) And we know that freedom is a gift from our Creator...

"And now I would like to ask a tremendous friend of all of ours, Pastor Paula White, to come up and bless our meal. Paula, please."

PASTOR PAULA WHITE: *"It's an honor to be here. And before we pray the prayer, this group would like to present to you and First Lady a Bible that is signed by over a hundred Christians, Evangelicals that love you, pray for you. And I'd just love to read the inscription for you and First Lady...*

"It says: 'First Lady and President, you are in our prayers always. Thank you for your courageous and bold stand for religious liberty, and for your timeless service to all Americans. We appreciate the price that you have paid to walk in the high calling. History will record the greatness that you have brought for generations.' (Prayer is given.)"[39]

1 SAMUEL 12:4

...for consider what GREAT things He has done for you.

September 7, 2018 — President Trump made a

Proclamation on National Days of Prayer and Remembrance, 2018.

THE PRESIDENT: *"During the National Days of Prayer and Remembrance, we pause to honor the memory of the nearly 3,000 innocent people who were murdered by radical Islamist terrorists in the brutal attacks of September 11, 2001. We come together to pray for those whose lives were forever changed by the loss of a loved one... Darkness, hatred, and death marred that fateful September morning, 17 years ago. Our Nation watched with stunned silence, tears, anger, and utter disbelief as multiple tragedies unfolded...*

"During these annual days of prayer and remembrance, we pray that all find peace in the love of God, courage to face the future, and comfort in the knowledge that those who were lost will never be forgotten."[40]

September 14, 2018 — President Trump proclaimed National Gang Violence Prevention Week, 2018.

THE PRESIDENT: *"While my Administration has successfully indicted and convicted countless gang members, gang violence still destroys families and threatens our liberty. When street gangs smuggle drugs into our communities, violence, addiction, overdoses, and other criminal activities follow. Extortion, sex trafficking, murder, robbery, and witness intimidation are only some of the evils that trail in the wake of gang activity...*

"I have also instructed my Administration to aggressively address transnational criminal organizations, especially MS-13. Organized and led from Central America, MS-13 has entrenched its claws in communities from the East Coast to the West Coast. Its growing influence poses a serious risk to our country's youth and community safety...

"This week, we rededicate ourselves to dismantling, and ultimately eradicating, criminal gang organizations, which threaten our way of life."[41]

PSALM 11:5 (NLT)

The LORD examines both the righteous and the wicked. He hates those who love violence.

October 6, 2018 — President Trump's second nominee to the US Supreme Court, Justice Brett Kavanaugh, was confirmed by the Senate. The confirmation hearings were among the nastiest in US history. Kavanaugh, like Gorsuch, is a constitutional originalist.

DEUTERONOMY 1:16-17

16 "Then I commanded your judges at that time, saying, 'Hear the cases between your brethren, and judge righteously between a man and his brother or the stranger who is with him.

17 You shall not show partiality in judgment; you shall hear the small as well as the great; you shall not be afraid in any man's presence, for the judgment is God's. The case that is too hard for you, bring to me, and I will hear it.'

ISAIAH 61:8 (CSB)

For I the LORD love justice; I hate robbery and injustice; I will faithfully reward my people and make a permanent covenant with them.

October 12, 2018 — President Trump announced successful negotiation for the release of Pastor Andrew Brunson from Turkish prison.

God honored the President because it was on this day that an article was published in *The Washington Examiner* listing 289 accomplishments of his presidency in the first 20 months (or 600 days). The columnist Paul Bedard concluded that Trump's "list of achievements had surpassed those of former President Ronald Reagan" and demonstrated "relentless promise-keeping."[42]

1 SAMUEL 2:30

...for those who honor Me I will honor, and those who despise Me shall be lightly esteemed.

October 13, 2018 — President Trump invited Pastor Andrew Brunson to the Oval Office and spoke on several hostage situations resolved under his Administration.

THE PRESIDENT: *"I was actually very surprised that we didn't work this out a couple of months ago. But it started in a different administration, and they were not going to work out anything. And we took it over, we inherited it. And we have, I think at this moment, gotten 19 different people out of various countries that were being held.*

"Chairman Kim was really great to us. I think that started the relationship that we have now in North Korea, with three hostages, as you know. Egypt—we had Aya. Aya was, they said, a spy. She was sentenced to 25 years. They told President Obama, "We will not let her out under any circumstances." And they told me, "She'll be in the Oval Office in 24 hours."

PASTOR BRUNSON: *"... we especially want to thank the administration. You really fought for us, unusually so. From the time you took office, I know that you've been engaged, and Secretary of State Pompeo also was very engaged and fought for us. And Vice President Pence, we're very grateful. Mr. Bolton.*

"There are a number of people in the Senate. And I can't mention everyone, but I know that Senator Tillis visited me in prison, and so did Senator Shaheen and Senator Graham. And Senator Lankford has been involved from the very beginning.

"So, we're so grateful to so many people in the Congress who stood with us and who prayed for us, and who fought for us..."

THE PRESIDENT: *"I think if there was ever a bipartisan event, this was it. And I do have to thank Vice President Pence. He's doing a terrific job. He felt very, very strongly about this. And*

Secretary of State Pompeo, I would say we spoke about this at least once a day."

PASTOR BRUNSON: *"We would like to pray for you. We pray for you often as a family. My wife and I pray for you." (Pastor and his wife offered a prayer for the President.)*[43]

HEBREWS 10:34 (ESV)

For you had compassion on those in prison...

November 7, 2018 — The Department of Health and Human Services (HHS) finalized its two regulations to protect conscience and religious liberty from long-standing problems with the Obamacare "contraceptive mandate." What were some of the problems?

In July 2015, an order of Catholic nuns called *Little Sisters of the Poor* lost an appeal to be exempt from having to provide government-approved contraceptives. The US Court of Appeals for the Tenth Circuit ordered *Little Sisters of the Poor* to comply to Obamacare rules because they "do not substantially burden plaintiffs' religious exercise or violate the plaintiffs' First Amendment rights."[44]

This ruling came despite the fact that one year earlier, the Supreme Court had issued a landmark decision in favor of *Hobby Lobby*, allowing closely held for-profit corporations to be exempt from a regulation its owners religiously objected to. It was the first time that the court recognized a for-profit corporation's claim of religious belief.[45]

The Trump Administration helped Christians bypass the onerous decision of the federal appeals court by changing the HHS rules. As reported by the Family Research Council: *"These two final regulations exempt organizations with either a moral or religious objection to purchasing insurance with coverage of contraceptives and abortion-causing drugs and devices. The regulations took effect on January 14, 2019."*[46]

Little Sisters of the Poor would eventually go on to win their case in the Supreme Court in July 2020, but only after an ordeal that stretched more than 5 years.

ECCLESIASTES 8:11

Because the sentence against an evil work is not executed speedily, therefore the heart of the sons of men is fully set in them to do evil.

One of the injustices of the European world was that its court system could harass an innocent person by dragging them through a long and painful process. Legal delays violated Ecclesiastes 8:11, which demands that justice must be swift.

The Founding Fathers loathed the corrupt European system, under which many of them suffered, and wrote the Sixth Amendment to the US Constitution to counteract judicial abuses. It provides that "in all criminal prosecutions, the accused shall enjoy the right to a speedy and public trial, by an impartial jury" of his peers. To further define what is a speedy trial, Congress passed in 1974 the Speedy Trial Act.[47]

JEREMIAH 21:12 (NLT)

This is what the LORD says to the dynasty of David: "Give justice each morning to the people you judge! Help those who have been robbed; rescue them from their oppressors. Otherwise, my anger will burn like an unquenchable fire because of all your sins.

December 18, 2018 — President Trump signed an Executive Order to give federal employees an extra day off on Christmas Eve.[48]

As the President promised on the campaign trail, he would bring the Christmas spirit back to Washington and Americans would be able to say "Merry Christmas!" again without fear of reprisal by employers or the government.

MATTHEW 2:1-2 (NIV)

After Jesus was born in Bethlehem in Judea, during the time of King Herod, Magi from the east came to Jerusalem and asked, "Where is the one who has been born king of the Jews? We saw his star when it rose and have come to worship him."

December 21, 2018 — President Trump signed the historic, bipartisan criminal justice reform legislation, called the First Step Act of 2018 (S. 756). It was one of the few things Republicans and Democrats could agree on in four years.

Criminal justice reform is a boon to the black community because it has suffered disproportionate incarceration. Many black men have been imprisoned for minor offenses or been made an example of in the failed war on drugs. Returning black men who are not guilty of violent crimes into the community and helping them to become productive members of society is one of the most pro-black achievements during President Trump's first term.

Rep. Hakeem Jeffries' website states: *"The legislation will propel formerly-incarcerated individuals toward success when they return home, while enacting targeted reforms that would improve public safety and reduce recidivism. It authorizes $375 million over five years to develop new programs, including education, vocational training and mental health counseling. Consequently, newly-released individuals will be positioned to successfully re-enter society.*

"With respect to sentencing reform, the FIRST STEP Act will increase public safety and engineer much-needed changes to draconian sentencing laws connected to the failed war on drugs. It modifies the three strikes law to make it more humane, increases judicial discretion to reduce sentences for low-level nonviolent drug

offenders and provides retroactive relief for thousands unjustly sentenced during the crack-cocaine era."[49]

MATTHEW 23:4 (ESV)

They tie up HEAVY BURDENS, hard to bear, and lay them on people's shoulders, but they themselves are not willing to move them with their finger.

ISAIAH 42:6-7 (NIV)

...I will keep you and will make you to be a covenant for the people and a light for the Gentiles, to OPEN eyes that are blind, to FREE captives from prison and to RELEASE from the dungeon those who sit in darkness.

CHAPTER 6

THIRD YEAR: 2019

JANUARY **8, 2019** — Trump signed into law the Frederick Douglass Trafficking Victims Prevention and Protection Reauthorization Act.

This bill establishes programs to combat human trafficking, forced labor, and the use of child soldiers. It also modifies existing programs to address such issues.[1]

PROVERBS 22:8

Whoever sows injustice reaps calamity, and the rod they wield in fury will be broken.

ISAIAH 61:8 (ESV)

For I the Lord love justice; I hate robbery and wrong; I will faithfully give them their recompense, and I will make an everlasting covenant with them.

January 9, 2019 — Trump signs into law the Trafficking Victims Protection Reauthorization Act (S. 1862). This bill modifies the criteria for evaluating whether countries are meeting the minimum standards for combatting human trafficking.[2]

DEUTERONOMY 10:18

He executes justice for the orphan and the widow, and shows His love for the alien by giving him food and clothing.

PSALM 146:9

The Lord protects the strangers; He supports the fatherless and the widow, but He thwarts the way of the wicked.

January 14, 2019 — President Trump signs into law Combating European Anti-Semitism Act of 2017.[3]

DEUTERONOMY 28:7 (NIV) The Lord will grant that the enemies who rise up against you will be defeated before you. They will come at you from one direction but flee from you in seven.

January 15, 2019 — President Trump issued a Proclamation on Religious Freedom Day, 2019

THE PRESIDENT: *"The Pilgrims who landed at Plymouth shared an experience common to many of America's first settlers: they had fled their home countries to escape religious persecution...*

"Unfortunately, the fundamental human right to religious freedom is under attack. Efforts to circumscribe religious freedom—or to separate it from adjoining civil liberties, like property rights or free speech—are on the rise. Over time, legislative and political attacks on religious freedom have given way to actual violence. Last October, we witnessed a horrific attack on the Tree of Life Synagogue in Pittsburgh, Pennsylvania— the deadliest attack on the Jewish community in our Nation's history. Tragically, attacks on people of faith and their houses of worship have increased in frequency in recent years.

"My Administration is taking action to protect religious liberty

and to seek justice against those who seek to abridge it. The Department of Justice is aggressively prosecuting those who use violence or threats to interfere with the religious freedom of their fellow Americans...

"Around the globe today, people are being persecuted for their faith by authoritarian dictatorships, terrorist groups, and other intolerant individuals. To address this tragic reality, last July, at my request, the Secretary of State convened the first-ever Ministerial to Advance Religious Freedom. We are listening to the voices of those risking their lives for their religious beliefs, and we are listening to the families of people who have died fighting for their fundamental right of conscience.

"Our Nation was founded on the premise that a just government abides by the "Laws of Nature and of Nature's God." As the Founders recognized, the Constitution protects religious freedom to secure the rights endowed to man by his very nature. On this day, we recognize this history and affirm our commitment to the preservation of religious freedom."[4]

GALATIANS 5:1

Stand fast therefore in the liberty by which Christ has made us free, and do not be entangled again with a yoke of bondage.

January 18, 2019 — President Trump issued a Proclamation on the National Sanctity of Human Life Day, 2019.

THE PRESIDENT: *"Today marks the 46th year since the United States Supreme Court's decision in Roe v. Wade. On this day, National Sanctity of Human Life Sunday, we mourn the lives cut short, and the tremendous promise lost, as a result of abortion. As a Nation, we must resolve to protect innocent human life at every stage.*

"As President, I am committed to defending the Right to Life. During my first week in office, I reinstated the Mexico City Policy,

which prevents foreign aid from being used to fund or support the global abortion industry. We are also working to end the abhorrent practice of elective late-term abortion, a practice allowed in only seven countries around the world.

"At home, we have issued a proposed regulation to implement the Title X prohibition on funding programs that include abortion as a method of family planning. I am supporting the effort in the United States Senate to make permanent the Hyde Amendment, which has been added year after year to spending bills and prevents taxpayer funding for abortion. And I have explicitly informed the Congress that I will veto any legislation that weakens existing Federal protections for human life."[5]

JEREMIAH 1:5

"Before I formed you in the womb I knew you; Before you were born I sanctified you..."

February 7, 2019 — President Trump attended the National Prayer Breakfast.

THE PRESIDENT: *"With us today are leaders involved with Prison Fellowship, started by the late Chuck Colson—a man transformed by leaders of this breakfast. Today, Prison Fellowship ministers to more than 300,000 prisoners across America to help others like Alice Johnson and Matthew Charles, who we saw Tuesday night, transform their lives through the mercy and grace of God.*

"And faith leaders helped us achieve historic bipartisan criminal justice reform. They've been wanting to do that for many, many years, and we all together got it done. We just passed the FIRST STEP Act into law. So thank you very much, everybody in the room, for that help. That was a very big thing for our country.

"America is a nation that believes in redemption. Every day, the people in this room demonstrate the power of faith to transform lives, heal communities, and lift up the forgotten...

"As President, I will always cherish, honor, and protect the believers who uplift our communities and sustain our nation.

"To ensure that people of faith can always contribute to our society, my administration has taken historic action to protect religious liberty.

"Here with us this morning are Melissa and Chad Buck from Holt, Michigan. In 2009, they decided to adopt. Soon, they got a call about three young siblings in a terribly abusive home. Melissa and Chad had only a few minutes to decide, and they said yes to all three. Today, the Bucks have five beautiful adopted children. As Melissa has said, 'They are the sweetest, most lovable children. They have the most unique gifts.' Two of them have joined us for this breakfast: 10-year-old Max and 9-year-old Liz.

"To Max, Liz, and the entire Buck family, thank you for inspiring us all...

"Unfortunately, the Michigan adoption charity that brought the Buck family together is now defending itself in court for living by the values of its Catholic faith. We will always protect our country's long and proud tradition of faith-based adoption. My administration is working to ensure that faith-based adoption agencies are able to help vulnerable children find their forever families, while following their deeply held beliefs.

"My administration is also speaking out against religious persecution around the world, including against religious minorities, Christians, and the Jewish community...

"My administration is also continuing to fight for American hostages who have been imprisoned overseas for their religious beliefs. Last October, we reached an agreement with Turkey to release Pastor Andrew Brunson, who is now free and joins us here this morning. Where is Andrew? (Applause.) He was there for a long time before I got there, and I said, 'You've got to let him out.' (Laughter.) 'You better let him out.' And they let you out. (Laughter.) It was a miracle. (Applause.)

"This Saturday, Pastor Brunson will walk his daughter down the

aisle. Wow, that's great. Congratulations. Was I invited? I don't know. Was I invited? (Laughter.)

"... So today, and every day, let us pray for the future of our country. Let us pray for the courage to pursue justice and the wisdom to forge peace."[6]

February 22, 2019 — The Trump Administration cut off funding for abortion by announcing that "it will not allow organizations that provide referrals for abortions to receive federal family-planning money, which implies a cut in funding for Planned Parenthood (the nation's largest abortion provider) unless they perform abortions in a separate facility and do not refer patients to it."[7]

MATTHEW 18:14 (ESV)

So it is not the will of my Father who is in heaven that one of these little ones should perish?

DEUTERONOMY 18:10

There shall not be found among you anyone who makes his son or his daughter pass through the fire, or one who practices witchcraft, or a soothsayer, or one who interprets omens, or a sorcerer,

February 28, 2019 — President Trump met for the second time the leader of North Korea Kim Jong Un at Hanoi, Vietnam. Vietnam is considered sympathetic to North Korea since both are communist. Kim demanded that all nuclear sanctions be lifted. The summit collapsed abruptly and a planned signing ceremony was canceled.

THE PRESIDENT: "Sometimes you have to walk and I think that was one of these times. We had some options. At this time we decided not to do any of the options. We'll see where that goes."[8]

ECCLESIASTES 3:1, 8

1 To everything there is a season, A time for every purpose under heaven:

8 A time to love, And a time to hate; A time of war, And a time of peace.

March 21, 2019 — President Trump signed an Executive Order to promote First Amendment rights on college campuses. It is well known that academia has been taken over by leftist faculty, but conservative students were safe for a while. In the last three years, conservative students and guest speakers have been increasingly harassed, attacked[9] and censored,[10] such as by having their events cancelled at public universities.

THE PRESIDENT: "*We reject oppressive speech codes, censorship, political correctness, and every other attempt by the hard left to stop people from challenging ridiculous and dangerous ideas. These ideas are dangerous. Instead, we believe in free speech, including online and including on campus.*"[11]

The order ties federal research and education grants to a university's commitment to protect their students' right to free speech. Michelle Hackman of *The Wall Street Journal* commented, "The directive is the latest move on the part of the Trump administration, which has been flexing unprecedented legal muscle to defend conservative students in free-speech lawsuits against their universities."[12]

GALATIANS 4:16

Have I therefore become your enemy because I tell you the truth?

March 25, 2019 — President Trump issued a Proclamation on Recognizing the Golan Heights as Part of the State of Israel.

THE PRESIDENT: "*The State of Israel took control of the*

Golan Heights in 1967 to safeguard its security from external threats. Today, aggressive acts by Iran and terrorist groups, including Hizbollah, in southern Syria continue to make the Golan Heights a potential launching ground for attacks on Israel. Any possible future peace agreement in the region must account for Israel's need to protect itself from Syria and other regional threats. Based on these unique circumstances, it is therefore appropriate to recognize Israeli sovereignty over the Golan Heights.

"NOW, THEREFORE, I, DONALD J. TRUMP, President of the United States of America, by virtue of the authority vested in me by the Constitution and the laws of the United States, do hereby proclaim that, the United States recognizes that the Golan Heights are part of the State of Israel."[13]

EXODUS 23:31 (ESV)

And I will set your border from the Red Sea to the Sea of the Philistines, and from the wilderness to the Euphrates, for I will give the inhabitants of the land into your hand, and you shall drive them out before you.

April 1, 2019 — President Trump celebrated a bi-partisan achievement made at the 2019 Prison Reform Summit and by the passing of the FIRST STEP Act in December 2018.

THE PRESIDENT: *"Today we're here to celebrate the truly extraordinary bipartisan —that's a very pleasant word—that's a pleasant word—achievement of the FIRST STEP Act. Very important. This landmark legislation will give countless current and former prisoners a second chance at life and a new opportunity to contribute to their communities, their states, and their nations.*

"... So, many people said... that criminal justice reform would never pass. But we came together as a group, we worked across party lines, and we got it done.

"... In less than four months, more than 500 people with unfair

sentences have been released from prison and are free to begin a new life. (Applause.)"[14]

May 2, 2019 — The Trump Administration's Department of Health and Human Services issued "a new rule protecting healthcare workers who decline on the basis of conscience or religious conviction to participate in procedures such as abortion or assisted suicide."[15]

ROMANS 12:18

If it is possible, as much as depends on you, live peaceably with all men.

This verse implies that there are times when you will not be able to live peaceably with some people who impose a false rule or harsh demand on you. Contrary to what many in the church teach today, the Bible does not demand our unconditional submission to Government.

Those who teach unlimited submission based on Romans 13 do not believe what they say, otherwise they would also teach that wives must submit to abusive husbands unconditionally, or church goers must submit to unreasonable pastors unconditionally. None of the people who preach "we must always obey government" believes "we must always obey the pastor!"

As a pastor, I find it odd that Christians would wish to submit unconditionally to politicians more than to their own pastors. Politicians are prone to use force and abuse power. At least pastors know God, know their congregants by name, and do not have a gun pointed at their parishioners' heads. When the Bible refers to "those who rule over you," it more often refers to church pastors and elders than to godless politicians.

HEBREWS 13:17

Obey those who rule over you, and be submissive, for

they watch out for your souls, as those who must give account. Let them do so with joy and not with grief, for that would be unprofitable for you.

May 2, 2019 — President Trump made remarks at the National Day of Prayer Service.

THE PRESIDENT: *"I'd like to begin by sending our prayers to the people of Venezuela in their righteous struggle for freedom. The brutal repression of the Venezuelan people must end and it must end soon. People are starving. They have no food. They have no water. And this was once one of the wealthiest countries in the world. So we wish them well. We'll be there to help, and we are there to help. Thank you.*

"Today, we give thanks for this magnificent country. And we proudly come together as one nation under God. (Applause.) And one of the things that Mike and I were discussing just a little while ago: People are so proud to be using that beautiful word, 'God.' And they're using the word 'God' again. And they're not hiding from it. And they're not being told to take it down. And they're not saying, 'We can't honor God.'

"'In God we trust.' So important...

"When I first started campaigning, people were not allowed or, in some cases, foolishly ashamed to be using on stores 'Merry Christmas,' 'Happy Christmas.' They'd say 'Happy Holidays.' They'd have red walls and you'd never see 'Christmas.' That was four years ago. Take a look at your stores nowadays. It's all 'Merry Christmas' again. (Applause.) 'Merry Christmas' again. They're proud of it.

"I always said, 'You're going to be saying, 'Merry Christmas' again. And that's what's happened...'"

"In recent months—it's been pretty tough—we've seen evil and hate-filled attacks on religious communities in the United States and all around the world. One month ago, three historically black churches were burned, tragically, in Louisiana.

"In Sri Lanka and New Zealand, hundreds of Christians and

Muslims were brutally murdered at their places of worship. In October, an anti-Semitic killer attacked the Tree of Life Synagogue in Pittsburgh. That was a horrible event. The First Lady and I went. To see that was not even believable.

"And last week, a gunman opened fire at a Synagogue in Poway, California, while Jewish families celebrated the last day of Passover. We mourn for the loss of one extraordinary member of that congregation, Lori Gilbert-Kay, who stood in front of the shooter and gave her life to protect her rabbi...

"We will fight with all of our strength and everything that we have in our bodies to defeat anti-Semitism, to end the attacks on the Jewish people, and to conquer all forms of persecution, intolerance, and hate. (Applause.)

"... Earlier this week, I took action to ensure that federal employees can take paid time off to observe religious holy days. And just today, we finalized new protections of conscience rights for physicians, pharmacists, nurses, teachers, students, and faith-based charities. (Applause.) ... It happened today.

"... In addition, I am committing to you today that my administration will preserve the central role of faith-based adoption and foster care agencies to care for vulnerable children, while following their deeply held beliefs. (Applause.) And those are words you probably never thought you'd ever hear.

"To give former inmates a second chance at life, we passed criminal justice reform. Ivanka, stand up. (Applause.) ... Now, for the first time, faith-based organizations can serve federal prisoners. They can take care of the people in and they can take care of prisoners as they get out...

"And we're also supporting faith-based addiction recovery programs because we understand the power of prayer. (Applause.) And I will say our First Lady has taken to this. It's incredible what she's done. And we're down 16 percent with opioids. Sixteen percent is a lot.

"... And as God promises in the Bible, 'Those who hope in the Lord

will renew their strength. They will soar on the wings like eagles. They will run and not grow weary. And they will walk and not be faint.' And that's something that Mike and I think about all the time. Right, Mike? (Laughter.)

"... People say, 'How do you get through that whole stuff? How do you go through those witch hunts and everything else?' And you know what we do, Mike? We just do it. Right? And we think about God. That's true. So thank you all very much.

"On this Day of Prayer, we once again place our hopes in the hands of our Creator."[16]

REVELATION 4:11 (ESV)

"Worthy are you, our Lord and God, to receive glory and honor and power, for you created all things, and by your will they existed and were created."

May 24, 2019 — President Trump issued a Proclamation on Prayer for Peace, Memorial Day.

THE PRESIDENT: *"As President Lincoln said in 1863 during the dedication of the Gettysburg National Military Cemetery: "It is for us the living, rather, to be dedicated here to the unfinished work which they who fought here have thus far so nobly advanced.*

"As we approach the 75th anniversary of D-Day, we proudly commemorate those heroic and honorable patriots who gave their all for the cause of freedom during some of history's darkest hours. Thousands of selfless members of our Armed Forces perished on the beaches of Normandy. They bravely gave their lives to pave the way for the Allied liberation of Europe and ultimately victory over the forces of evil. Their historic sacrifices and achievements secured the future of humanity and proved America's strength in defending freedom and defeating the enemies of civilization."[17]

June 25, 2019 — President Trump appointed Dr. Ben Carson as Chair of a newly established White House Council on Eliminating Barriers to Affordable Housing Development.

Members from 8 Federal agencies are currently tasked with tearing down red tape in order to build more affordable housing. This is because 25% of the cost of a new home is the direct result of Federal, State, and local regulations, with some price tags reaching up to 42% for new multifamily construction.

THE PRESIDENT: *"We're lifting up forgotten communities, creating exciting new opportunities, and helping every American find their path to the American Dream."*[18]

NEHEMIAH 5:7 (NKJ)

After serious thought, I rebuked the nobles and rulers, and said to them, "Each of you is exacting usury [unreasonable interest] **from his brother." So I called a great assembly against them.**

June 30, 2019 — President Trump became the first sitting president to cross the 1953 armistice line separating North and South Korea, the first president to walk in the no-go demilitarized zone, and the first president to step into North Korea. He met Kim Jong Un for the third time in his presidency and the two had a 50-minute talk.

THE PRESIDENT tweeted the same day, 8:21pm: "Leaving South Korea after a wonderful meeting with Chairman Kim Jong Un. Stood on the soil of North Korea, an important statement for all, and a great honor!"[19]

JAMES 4:1-3

1 Where do wars and fights come from among you? Do they not come from your desires for pleasure that war in your members?

2 You lust and do not have. You murder and covet and cannot obtain. You fight and war. Yet you do not have because you do not ask.

3 You ask and do not receive, because you ask amiss, that you may spend it on your pleasures.

In pastoring for twenty years, I learned that people fuss, fight and manipulate others because they want something but don't know how to express it in a healthy way. I tell my children, it's not wrong to say what you want, but once you say it, it's up to the other person whether or not they will give it. But it's not wrong to express your pure desire. This message is one my church members' favorite: *Pure Desire, The Secret to Intimacy.*[20]

July 7, 2019 — In a Wall Street Journal op-ed, Secretary of State Mike Pompeo announced the creation of the Commission on Unalienable Rights.[21] The Secretary explained that the commission will examine the definition of human rights because the phrase has grown vague since the United Nations adopted the Universal Declaration of Human Rights in 1948. Mr. Pompeo suggested that human rights discourse had become corrupted, hijacked and used for dubious or malignant purposes.[22]

As a pastor, I have observed that religious liberties, freedom of speech, and children's rights to both parents are among human rights that are routinely violated in Western democracies. Mr. Pompeo's focus on this issue was refreshing to see and an important step to rectify an old document that has been weakened at best.

ISAIAH 6:8 (NIV)

Then I heard the voice of the Lord saying, "Whom shall I send? And who will go for us?" Then said I, "Here am I; send me."

July 16-18, 2019 — Secretary of State Mike Pompeo hosted the second Ministerial to Advance Religious Freedom in Washington. With more than 1,000 civil society and religious leaders from 106 countries participating, the 2019 Ministerial was the largest religious freedom event of its kind in the world.

MIKE POMPEO: *"The protection of religious freedom is central to the Trump administration's foreign policy, and protecting this human right is an essential part of who we are as Americans."*[23]

THE VICE PRESIDENT: *"The President made a bold statement in support of religious liberty when he appointed a friend and a lifelong champion of our first freedom as our Ambassador-at-Large for International Religious Freedom. And that man has now traveled the world, and his good work is evidenced in the historic turnout today. Would you all join me in recognizing and thanking Ambassador Sam Brownback for his work on behalf of religious liberty around the world?*

The list of religious freedom violators is long; their oppressions span the globe... In Venezuela, the dictator Nicolás Maduro is using his so-called "anti-hate" laws to prosecute Catholic clergy who speak out against his brutal regime that has impoverished millions in this once-prosperous country...

The Iranian people enjoy few, if any, freedoms — least of all, the freedom of religion. Christians, Jews, Sunnis, Bahá'ís, and other religious minorities are denied the most basic rights enjoyed by the Shia majority. And believers are routinely fined, flogged, and arrested in Iran. But the people of the United States of America have a message to the long-suffering people of Iran: Even as we stand strong against the leaders in Tehran, know that we are with you. We pray for you."[24]

PROVERBS 29:2 (NLT)

When the godly are in authority, the people rejoice. But when the wicked are in power, they groan.

July 17, 2019 — President Trump met 27 survivors of religious persecution from 17 countries.

Among them were North Carolina pastor Andrew Brunson

who was freed from a Turkish prison in 2018, and Mariam Ibrahim, a Christian mother who was freed from death row in Sudan in 2014.

From the Oval Office, the President encouraged the survivors: "*... we have a very important group of people standing alongside of me. I'm honored to welcome Pastor Andrew Brunson and other survivors of religious persecution to the White House... With us today are men and women of many different religious traditions from many different countries. But what you have in common is each of you has suffered tremendously for your faith: you've endured harassment, threats, attacks, trials, imprisonment and torture. Each of you has become a witness to the importance of advancing religious liberty all around the world. It's about religious liberty.*

"Last year, my administration hosted the world's first-ever meeting of foreign ministers devoted solely to the subject of international religious freedom. I want to thank all of you for joining us as we host this meeting for the second year in a row. A lot of individual breakout meetings are being had, and we're getting a lot of ideas as to how we can help.

"In America, we've always understood that ***our rights come from God, not from government.*** *In our Bill of Rights, the first liberty is religious liberty. Each of us has the right to follow the dictates of our conscience and the demands of our religious conviction. We know that if people are not free to practice their faith, then all of the freedoms are at risk and, frankly, freedoms don't mean very much.*

"That's why Americans will never tire in our effort to defend and promote religious freedom. I don't think any President has taken it as seriously as me. To me, it's very important. It's vital."[25]

2 Samuel 23:3

...He who rules over men must be just...

Rulers and nations are judged when they forget that there is a King over their kingdoms. Nebuchadnezzar was used of God to judge many sinful nations, including Israel, but when he fell into pride, the prophet Daniel reminded him that God watches every leader on earth and holds them accountable.

DANIEL 4:25

...you shall be driven from among men, and your dwelling shall be with the beasts of the field. You shall be made to eat grass like an ox, and you shall be wet with the dew of heaven, and seven periods of time (7 years) **shall pass over you, TILL YOU KNOW that the Most High rules the kingdom of men and gives it to whom he will.**

July 29, 2019 — President Trump commuted the sentence of Ronen Nahmani, an Israeli born man who had served 4 of his 20-year sentence for conspiracy to distribute synthetic drugs he bought from China.

His 10-year-old daughter Oriel wrote the President: *"My mom is always sad and cries," Oriel's letter read, according to Ynet. "She is always sick and doesn't have strength. Today's my birthday. I am 10 and half of my life I had no dad. Please let my dad come."*[26]

THE PRESIDENT: *"Mr. Nahmani is a non-violent, first-time offender with no criminal history. He has five young children at home and his wife is suffering from terminal cancer. These extenuating circumstances underscore the urgency of his request for clemency."*[27]

2 SAMUEL 9:3 (NIV)

The king (David) **asked, "Is there no one still alive from the house of Saul to whom I can SHOW GOD'S KINDNESS?" Ziba answered the king, "There is still a son of Jonathan; he is lame in both feet."**

September 5, 2019 — President Trump issued a Proclamation on National Days of Prayer and Remembrance.

THE PRESIDENT: *"During these National Days of Prayer and Remembrance, we come together to honor the memory of the nearly 3,000 men, women, and children who perished in the terrorist attacks of September 11, 2001. The passage of time will never diminish the magnitude of the loss or the courage, compassion, strength, and unity displayed during one of our darkest hours.*

"Since the founding of our Republic, we have proclaimed reliance on Almighty God. Prayer has sustained and guided the leaders and citizens of this great Nation in times of peace and prosperity and in times of conflict and disaster. Thus, it is fitting that we again turn to our Creator for wisdom, comfort, and peace on this somber occasion, praying for those who lost loved ones at the World Trade Center, at the Pentagon, and in Shanksville, Pennsylvania, and for all who bear the wounds, seen and unseen, of these tragedies."[28]

One of the human tragedies is that people so easily forget. 9/11 changed the world. It was the greatest act of terrorism on American soil. No adult who saw it could forget the day. But a new generation has been born and grown up without any remembrance of this event.

The Bible exists to remind us of the most important events to have ever transpired in human history.

PSALM 102:12

But thou, O Lord, shalt endure for ever; and thy remembrance unto all generations.

September 23, 2019 — President Trump became the first president to host a United Nations event on religious freedom. Speaking from the United Nations Headquarters in New York City,

THE PRESIDENT: *"Today, it's a true honor to be the first President of the United States to host a meeting at the United Nations on religious freedom. And an honor it is. It's long overdue. And I was shocked when I was given that statistic that I would be the first. I want to thank Vice President Pence for the outstanding job he's doing...*

"The Johnson Amendment doesn't get spoken about enough, but I'm very proud to say that we've obliterated the Johnson Amendment within our country so that now we can listen to the people that we want to listen to—religious leaders—without recrimination against them...

"The United States is founded on the principle that our rights do not come from government; they come from God. This immortal truth is proclaimed in our Declaration of Independence and enshrined in the First Amendment to our Constitution's Bill of Rights. Our Founders understood that no right is more fundamental to a peaceful, prosperous, and virtuous society than the right to follow one's religious convictions.

"Regrettably, the religious freedom enjoyed by American citizens is rare in the world. Approximately 80 percent of the world's population live in countries where religious liberty is threatened, restricted, or even banned. And when I heard that number, I said, 'Please go back and check it because it can't possibly be correct.' And, sadly, it was. Eighty percent.

"Today, with one clear voice, the United States of America calls upon the nations of the world to end religious persecution. (Applause.) To stop the crimes against people of faith, release prisoners of conscience, repeal laws restricting freedom of religion and belief, protect the vulnerable, the defenseless, and the oppressed. America stands with believers in every country who ask only for the freedom to live according to the faith that is within their own hearts.

"As President, protecting religious freedom is one of my highest priorities and always has been. Last year, our Secretary of State, Mike Pompeo, hosted the first-ever Ministerial to Advance International Religious Freedom.

"In this year's ministerial, Secretary Pompeo announced plans to create the International Religious Freedom Alliance—an alliance of

likeminded nations devoted to confronting religious persecution all around the world...

"It is estimated that 11 Christians are killed every day for the following—I mean, just think of this: Eleven Christians a day, for following the teachings of Christ. Who would even think that's possible in this day and age? Who would think it's possible?

"With us today is Pastor Andrew Brunson, who was imprisoned in Turkey for a long period of time. Last year, my administration was thrilled to bring him back home after a very short and respectful negotiation with a very strong man—and a man who has become a friend of mine, fortunately—President Erdoğan of Turkey.

"I called the President, and I said, 'He's an innocent man.' They've been trying to get Andrew out for a long time—previous administration. I don't think they tried too hard, unfortunately.

"... And I also want to thank Franklin Graham because he's been so instrumental in everything we're doing. He's done such an incredible job in so many different ways, including floods and hurricanes. And every time I go, I see Franklin there. He's always there before me. I don't know how he gets there before me. I'm going to beat him one day...

"In recent times, the world has also witnessed devastating acts of violence in sacred places of worship. In 2016, an 85-year-old Catholic priest was viciously killed while celebrating mass in Normandy, France. In the past year, the United States endured horrifying anti-Semitic attacks against Jewish Americans at synagogues in Pennsylvania and California. In March, Muslims praying with their families were sadistically murdered in New Zealand. On Easter Sunday this year, terrorists bombed Christian churches in Sri Lanka, killing hundreds of faithful worshippers. Who would believe this is even possible? These evil attacks are a wound on all humanity...

"The United States is forming a coalition of US businesses for the protection of religious freedom. This is the first time this has been done. This initiative will encourage the private sector to protect people of all faiths in the workplace. And the private sector has

brilliant leadership. And that's why some of the people in this room are among the most successful men and women on earth.

"... no force on earth is stronger than the faith of religious believers. The United States of America will forever remain at your side and the side of all who seek religious freedom."[29]

MICAH 1:17

Learn to do good;
Seek justice,
Rebuke the oppressor;
Defend the fatherless,
Plead for the widow.

October 18, 2019 — President Trump issued a Memorandum on Determination with Respect to the Efforts of Foreign Governments Regarding Trafficking in Persons.

By this, the United States will cease to provide non-humanitarian aid, nontrade-related assistance, and/or loans during the fiscal year 2020 to nations that do not meet the minimum standards for the elimination of trafficking in persons. The memorandum names violators, including the Governments of Belarus, Bhutan, Burundi, China, Comoros, Cuba, the Democratic People's Republic of Korea (DPRK), Equatorial Guinea, Eritrea, The Gambia, Iran, Mauritania, Papua New Guinea (PNG), Russia, Saudi Arabia, South Sudan, Syria, Turkmenistan, and Venezuela.[30]

PSALM 119:134 (ESV)

Redeem me from man's oppression, that I may keep your precepts.

October 27, 2019 — Abu Bakr al-Baghdadi, the founder and leader of ISIS, was brought to justice. In Operation Kayla Mueller (named after a 26-year-old humanitarian aid worker who was abducted in 2013, tortured and sexually abused by al-Baghdadi until she died in 2015), a dog named Conan chased the ISIS leader down a tunnel. Cornered in a dead end, he detonated a suicide belt, killing himself and two children. His death signaled the end of ISIS was near.

PSALM 143:12

In Your mercy cut off my enemies, And destroy all those who afflict my soul; For I am Your servant.

November 8, 2019 — President Trump proclaimed World Freedom Day on November 9, 2019.

THE PRESIDENT: *"For more than 10,000 days, the Berlin Wall stood as a troubling reminder of a deeply divided world, an evil obstacle to freedom and individual liberty. When the wall finally came down, it marked a triumphant defeat of communism, a monumental victory for democratic principles, and a righteous end to the nearly five-decades-long Cold War. On World Freedom Day, we remember those who suffered as they longed for freedom behind the Iron Curtain, and we recognize those relentlessly fighting today to break free from the shackles of oppression.*

"Any system of government that impedes the God-given rights of the people is destined to fail because the flame of liberty cannot be extinguished. As President Ronald Reagan said at the Brandenburg Gate in West Berlin, "The totalitarian world produces backwardness because it does such violence to the spirit, thwarting the human impulse to create, to enjoy, to worship."[31]

The division of a nation into two has not only happened to North and South Korea, North and South Vietnam, and East and West Germany, but also to North and South Israel. It is a main theme of the Old Testament and is called The Great Divorce by some theologians.[32]

After the reign of King Solomon the Wise, his son Rehoboam foolishly oppressed his people and imposed high taxes. The United Kingdom of Israel split into two. The northern part was called Israel (or Ephraim) with its capital in Samaria. The southern part was called Judah with its capital in Jerusalem.

In each case, the longing of the citizens was to be reunified. Families were or are torn apart by such political divisions. The unwise decisions of self-interested politicians impacted the lives of people whether or not they were interested in politics. In the case of Israel's divorce from Judah, the Bible is clear about the underlying cause: the people had fallen into sin, idolatry and sexual immorality. As they did not honor God as their leader, God gave them up to unwise leaders.

ISAIAH 3:4 (God's Word)

"I will make boys their leaders. Children will govern them." People will oppress each other, and everyone will oppress his neighbor. The young will make fun of the old, and common people will make fun of their superiors.

One of the features of communism is that initially it is led by young people. A sign that a nation is under the curse is that it is governed by young people. The Bible does not say that young people cannot rule or even rule well—King Josiah was a youth when he became king and he led Israel in revival. God called Samuel and Jeremiah when both were in their youth. But the Bible teaches that a government composed mostly of young people is easily misguided. It lacks the depth and diversity that older leaders with experience bring.

One modern example is Finland, where in 2019, 34 years-old Sanna Marin became the world's youngest prime minister. On its own, this fact could be considered a personal achievement, but her Minister of Finance, Minister of Education, and Minister of Interior were all under 35. The left-controlled media touts this as an unqualified cause for celebration. Of course it is to them.

It is no secret that young people tend to be idealistic and vote for big government and against traditions. As they grow their families and wealth, they tend to become more conservative and vote for small government and for pro-life, pro-family policies. Benjamin Disraeli (1804-1881) famously said, **"A man who is not a Liberal at sixteen has no heart; a man who is not a Conservative at sixty has no head."** Donald Trump is the perfect example of this. As a young man he was pro-abortion and supported Democrats; as he grew older and had more experience, he became pro-life and supported Republicans.

Age was a big factor in the minds of the Founding Fathers, otherwise they would not have put it in Article II of the US Constitution. No person under the age of 35 is legally qualified to be President. Why did they choose 35? Why not 40? Or 50? Looking back in American history, one can see that by 35, a person would have been sufficiently independent and mature to be married with children. Given today's trends in delayed maturation, the Founding Fathers might have increased the age of candidacy to 45 today.

The unrepresentative nature of the Finnish government spells trouble for the country's future. Unknown to many Americans, the Finnish government routinely cracks down on religious liberty. It is currently persecuting one of its female Parliamentarians, Päivi Räsänen, for publicly expressing her Bible-based views on marriage. MP Räsänen is married to a pastor and believes in the traditional family. She has not expressed any homophobic sentiment, but affirms the Biblical view that all humans—whether heterosexuals or homosexuals —are sinners who need to be saved by the Savior Jesus Christ. As of this writing, MP Räsänen has been under 4 separate police investigations for holding Biblical views that allegedly "defame homosexuals and commit agitation against an ethnic group." Her case and others are documented in chapter 10 of my book *Trump's Unfinished Business,* titled "Religious Liberty and Pink Communism."[33]

November 19, 2019 — The White House Press Secretary announced the release of two Hostages from the Taliban.

THE PRESS SECRETARY: *"Today, the United States welcomes the release of Professors Kevin King and Timothy Weeks. King, an American, and Weeks, an Australian, were professors at the American University of Afghanistan when they were kidnapped at gunpoint in August 2016.*

"Both men were successfully recovered today and are currently receiving medical care and other support from the United States Government. We pray for the full recovery of both men, who endured significant hardship during their captivity, and wish them well as they reunite with their loved ones in the near future."[34]

PSALM 146:7 (ESV)

Who executes justice for the oppressed, who gives food to the hungry. The Lord sets the prisoners free;

December 9, 2019 — President Trump proclaimed December 10, 2019, as Human Rights Day; December 15, 2019, as Bill of Rights Day; and the week beginning on December 8, 2019, as Human Rights Week.

THE PRESIDENT: *"Jefferson famously wrote to Madison: 'A bill of rights is what the people are entitled to against every government on earth, general or particular, and what no just government should refuse or rest on inference.' In the 228 years since the adoption of the Bill of Rights, it has continuously served as the guarantor of some of our most cherished freedoms: the right to practice the religion we choose, the right to speak freely and openly, the right to privacy, and the right to keep and bear arms.*

"Since taking office, I have worked to confine government

authority to its proper, constitutional scope. In May of 2017, I signed an Executive Order defending religious freedom and freedom of speech to better protect the First Amendment rights of all Americans. I signed another Executive Order in March to promote free speech on college campuses, protecting free inquiry and open debate at universities across the country. These orders recognize that freedom of speech is a fundamental right that must always be guarded vigilantly."[35]

PSALM 118:17

I shall not die, but live, And declare the works of the Lord.

December 19, 2019 — President Trump signed the Future Act, a bipartisan bill to restore funding to Historically Black Colleges and Universities (HBCU). It permanently provides $255 million a year to HBCUs and other minority-serving institutions.

Where did the government get this money from? By simplifying the form students use to determine their eligibility for federal aid, the Free Application for Federal Student Aid (FAFSA)—by eliminating 22 out of the 108 questions on the forms—the government estimates that it will save $2.8 billion over 10 years, money that will be re-directed to funding higher education for minorities.

The bill also eliminates the duplicate verification process, whereby families had to give their same tax information to the federal government twice—first to the IRS, then again to the US Department of Education.[36] Reducing the size of government forms and red tape spells real savings to taxpayers and real benefits to students.

THE PRESIDENT: "*When I took office, I promised to fight for HBCUs, and my administration continues to deliver. A few months ago, funding for HBCUs was in jeopardy. But the White House and Congress came together and reached a historic agreement."*[37]

ISAIAH 58:6

"Is this not the fast that I have chosen: To loose the bonds of wickedness, To UNDO the HEAVY BURDENS, To let the oppressed go free, And that you break every yoke?

December 31, 2019 — President Trump issued a Proclamation on National Slavery and Human Trafficking Prevention Month.

THE PRESIDENT: *"Human trafficking is often a hidden crime that knows no boundaries. By some estimates, as many as 24.9 million people—adults and children—are trapped in a form of modern slavery around the world, including in the United States. Human traffickers exploit others through forced labor or commercial sex, and traffickers profit from their victims' horrific suffering. The evil of human trafficking must be defeated.*

"... In January 2019, I was proud to sign both the Frederick Douglass Trafficking Victims Prevention and Protection Reauthorization Act and the Trafficking Victims Protection Reauthorization Act, reaffirming our commitment to preventing trafficking in all forms.

"... the Department of Homeland Security initiated more than 800 investigations related to human trafficking... in Fiscal Year 2018 [HHS] funded victim assistance programs that provided benefits and services to more than 2,400 victims. For the first time, the Department of Transportation committed $5.4 million in grants to the prevention of human trafficking and other crimes that may occur on buses, trains, and other forms of public transportation."[38]

PSALM 119:134 (ESV)

Redeem me from man's oppression, that I may keep your precepts.

CHAPTER 7

FOURTH YEAR: 2020

JANUARY 3, 2020 — President Trump announced that a US airstrike in Iraq killed the Iranian Revolutionary Guard General Qasem Soleimani.

THE PRESIDENT at Mar-a-Lago: "*Last night at my direction the United States military successfully executed a flawless precision strike that killed the No.1 terrorist anywhere in the world...We took action last night to stop a war. We did not take action to start a war.*"[1]

DEUTERONOMY 28:7 (NIV)

The Lord will grant that the enemies who rise up against you will be defeated before you. They will come at you from one direction but flee from you in seven.

January 15, 2020 — President Trump issued a Proclamation on Religious Freedom Day.

THE PRESIDENT: "*Religious freedom in America, often referred to as our 'first freedom,' was a driving force behind some of the earliest defining moments of our American identity. The desire for religious freedom impelled the Pilgrims to leave their homes in Europe and journey to a distant land, and it is the reason so many others seeking to live out their faith or change their faith have made America their home...*

"Since I took office, my Administration has been committed to protecting religious liberty. In May 2017, I signed an Executive Order to advance religious freedom for individuals and institutions, and I stopped the Johnson Amendment from interfering with pastors' right to speak their minds. Over the last 3 years, the Department of Justice has obtained 14 convictions in cases involving attacks or threats against places of worship...

"Repressive governments persecute religious worshipers using high-tech surveillance, mass detention, and torture, while terrorist organizations carry out barbaric violence against innocent victims on account of their religion. To cast a light on these abuses, in July 2019, I welcomed survivors of religious persecution from 16 countries into the Oval Office...

"I... do hereby proclaim January 16, 2020, as Religious Freedom Day. I call on all Americans to commemorate this day with events and activities that remind us of our shared heritage of religious liberty and that teach us how to secure this blessing both at home and around the world."[2]

In the Bible, not all Israel's leaders valued religion. Not all wanted to put God first and obey the Bible. Only a few courageous leaders defended the free exercise of religion or promoted it as a benefit to a strong, peaceful nation.

NEHEMIAH 13:11

So I contended with the rulers, and said, "Why is the house of God forsaken?" And I gathered them together and set them in their place.

The Good News Translations says:

I reprimanded the officials for letting the Temple be neglected...

JANUARY 21, 2020 — President Trump issued a Proclamation on National Sanctity of Human Life Day

THE PRESIDENT: *"My Administration has also issued regulations to ensure Title X family planning projects are clearly separated from those that perform, promote, or refer for abortion as a method of family planning; to protect the conscience rights of healthcare workers and organizations, including with respect to abortion; and to ensure the Federal Government does not force employers that object, based on religious belief or moral conviction, to provide insurance for contraceptives, including those they believe cause early abortions. Additionally, I have called on the Congress to act to prohibit abortions of later-term babies who can feel pain.*

"My Administration is also building an international coalition to dispel the concept of abortion as a fundamental human right. So far, 24 nations representing more than a billion people have joined this important cause. We oppose any projects that attempt to assert a global right to taxpayer-funded abortion on demand, up to the moment of delivery. And we will never tire of defending innocent life —at home or abroad.

"I... do hereby proclaim January 22, 2020, as National Sanctity of Human Life Day. Today, I call on the Congress to join me in protecting and defending the dignity of every human life, including those not yet born. I call on the American people to continue to care for women in unexpected pregnancies and to support adoption and foster care in a more meaningful way, so every child can have a loving home. And finally, I ask every citizen of this great Nation to ***listen to the sound of silence*** *caused by a generation lost to us, and then to raise their voices for all affected by abortion, both seen and unseen."*[3]

ISAIAH 49:15 (ESV)

"Can a woman forget her nursing child, that she should

have no compassion on the son of her womb? Even these may forget, yet I will not forget you.

January 21, 2020 — Trump was invited for a second time to attend the 50th anniversary of Davos or the World Economic Forum. His full speech has been buried by search engines. I could not find it using exact word search except at the White House's official website. Media outlets roasted the President with headlines that read: "Trump snubs Davos vision in another America-first speech"[4] and "Trump's speech at Davos is putting chill down European spines."[5]

This was the President's strongest rebuke of Global Warming/ Climate Change's political agenda, delivered hours before the teenage activist Greta Thunberg would deliver her rebuke to world leaders for doing "basically nothing"[6] to reduce carbon, an element that is essential to life, to plants, and makes up only 0.04% of the planet's atmosphere.

THE PRESIDENT: *"We've regained our stride, we discovered our spirit and reawakened the powerful machinery of American enterprise. America is thriving, America is flourishing, and yes, America is winning again like never before.*

"Just last week alone, the United States concluded two extraordinary trade deals: the agreement with China and the United States-Mexico-Canada Agreement — the two biggest trade deals ever made. They just happened to get done in the same week.

"These agreements represent a new model of trade for the 21st century — agreements that are fair, reciprocal, and that prioritize the needs of workers and families...

"For the first time in decades, we are no longer simply concentrating wealth in the hands of a few. We're concentrating and creating the most inclusive economy ever to exist. We are lifting up Americans of every race, color, religion, and creed...

"Workers' wages are now growing faster than management wages. Earnings growth for the bottom 10 percent is outpacing the top 10 percent — something that has not happened.... ***This is a blue-collar boom.***

"Since my election, the net worth of the bottom half of wage earners has increased by plus-47 percent — three times faster than the increase for the top 1 percent. Real median household income is at the highest level ever recorded. ***The American Dream is back...***

"The time for skepticism is over. People are flowing back into our country. Companies are coming back into our country...America achieved this stunning turnaround not by making minor changes to a handful of policies, but by adopting a whole new approach centered entirely on the wellbeing of the American worker.

"Every decision we make — on taxes, trade, regulation, energy, immigration, education, and more — is focused on improving the lives of everyday Americans. We are determined to create the highest standard of living that anyone can imagine, and right now, that's what we're doing for our workers. The highest in the world. A ***nation's highest duty is to its own citizens.***

"Today, I hold up the American model as an example to the world of a working system of free enterprise that will produce the most benefits for the most people in the 21st century and beyond.

"A ***pro-worker, pro-citizen, pro-family agenda*** *demonstrates how a nation can thrive when its communities, its companies, its government, and its people work together for the good of the whole nation.*

"...Before I was elected, China's predatory practices were undermining trade for everyone, but no one did anything about it, except allow it to keep getting worse and worse and worse. Under my leadership, America confronted the problem head on..."[7]

It's no surprise this speech was buried by the Internet. They don't want you to know America is winning again. After comparing America's *real success* to the globalist dream of a one world utopia (a dream that has failed and put people in misery and under tyranny time and time again), Trump addressed the fanatics of global warming / climate change.

THE PRESIDENT: *"I'm proud to report the United States has among the cleanest air and drinking water on Earth — and we're going to keep it that way. And we just came out with a report that, at this moment, it's the cleanest it's been in the last 40 years. We're committed to conserving the majesty of God's creation and the natural beauty of our world.*

"Today, I'm pleased to announce the United States will join One Trillion Trees Initiative being launched here at the World Economic Forum. One Trillion Trees. (Applause.) And in doing so, we will continue to show strong leadership in restoring, growing, and better managing our trees and our forests.

"This is not a time for pessimism; this is a time for optimism. Fear and doubt is not a good thought process because this is a time for tremendous hope and joy and optimism and action.

"But to embrace the possibilities of tomorrow, ***we must reject the perennial prophets of doom and their predictions of the apocalypse.*** *They are the heirs of yesterday's* ***foolish fortune-tellers*** *— and I have them and you have them, and we all have them, and they want to see us do badly, but we don't let that happen.* ***They predicted an overpopulation crisis in the 1960s, mass starvation in the '70s, and an end of oil in the 1990s.*** *These alarmists always demand the same thing:* ***absolute power*** *to dominate, transform, and control every aspect of our lives.*

"We will never let radical socialists destroy our economy, wreck our country, or eradicate our liberty. America will always be the proud, strong, and unyielding bastion of freedom."[8]

Remember the goal of globalism dates back to the Biblical Tower of Babel. Any human who thinks he can or should rule the whole world is, by definition, a megalomaniac. What if someone or some nations wants to be free from his control, his dictates, his laws? The only way such a globalist can achieve his global unity is by force—be it legal force, police force or military force. The Bible teaches that God made sovereign nations, separated by mutually unintelligible languages, in order to protect people from suffering under one world dictator.

GENESIS 11:3-4, 8-9

3 Then they said to one another, "Come, let us make bricks and bake them thoroughly." They had brick for stone, and they had asphalt for mortar.

4 And they said, "Come, let us build ourselves a city, and a tower whose top is in the heavens; let us make a name for ourselves, lest we be scattered abroad over the face of the whole earth."

8 So the Lord scattered them abroad from there over the face of all the earth, and they ceased building the city.

9 Therefore its name is called Babel, because there the Lord confused the language of all the earth...

January 24, 2020 — Trump became the first president to attend the March for Life in Washington, D.C. The first March for Life was held on January 22, 1974. In all those years, no sitting president had ever attended the March, although Republican presidents had normally sent written statements of support.

THE PRESIDENT: "*Young people are the heart of the March for Life, and it's your generation that is making America the pro-family, pro-life nation.*

"The life movement is led by strong women, amazing faith leaders, and brave students who carry on the legacy of pioneers before us who fought to raise the conscience of our nation and uphold the rights of our citizens. You embrace mothers with care and compassion. You are powered by prayer, and motivated by pure, unselfish love...

"When we see the image of a baby in the womb, we glimpse the

majesty of God's creation. When we hold a newborn in our arms, we know the endless love that each child brings to a family. When we watch a child grow, we see the splendor that radiates from each human soul. One life changes the world.

"I notified Congress that I would veto any legislation that weakens pro-life policies or that encourages the destruction of human life.

"At the United Nations, I made clear that global bureaucrats have no business attacking the sovereignty of nations that protect innocent life.

"Unborn children have never had a stronger defender in the White House. And as the Bible tells us, each person is 'wonderfully made.'"[9]

EXODUS 20:13

You shall not murder.

January 29, 2020 — Trump signed the "United States–Mexico–Canada Agreement" (USMCA) trade deal, which replaced the outdated NAFTA agreement proposed by Ronald Reagan in 1980, negotiated by George H. W. Bush in 1992, and signed by Bill Clinton in 1993.

What took other politicians 13 years to implement, Donald Trump took two years to dismantle and renegotiate.

THE PRESIDENT: *"The USMCA is the largest, most significant, modern, and balanced trade agreement in history. All of our countries will benefit greatly."*[10]

PROVERBS 10:22

The blessing of the Lord makes one rich, And He adds no sorrow with it.

January 31, 2020 — President issued an Executive Order on

Combating Human Trafficking and Online Child Exploitation in the United States.

PSALM 146:9 (CSB)

The LORD protects resident aliens and helps the fatherless and the widow, but he frustrates the ways of the wicked.

January 31, 2020 — One month after the first cluster of patients with COVID19 were infected in Wuhan, China, President Trump took swift action against an outbreak that had been covered up and allowed to spread worldwide by the Chinese Communist Party. He declared coronavirus a "public health emergency," announced Chinese travel restrictions and suspended entry into the United States for foreign nationals who pose a risk of transmitting the coronavirus. The Department of Homeland Security funneled all flights from China into just 7 domestic US airports.[11]

February 2, 2020 — Trump banned non-US citizens who recently visited China from entering the United States.

NUMBERS 5:2

"Command the sons of Israel that they send away from the camp every leper and everyone having a discharge and everyone who is unclean because of a dead person.

The Bible tells us how to deal with the most dreaded disease of the ancient times—leprosy. You quarantine the sick, not the healthy. You keep the infected and the exposed outside of the camp, for a set period of time or until they show no more symptoms.

Keeping people from the origin of the infection out of the United States made Biblical sense. But by March 2020, medical doctors experimented with something that had never been done before in human history, until the year 2020: quarantining healthy people inside their homes, closing churches, and shutting businesses down globally. By September 2020, *The Wall Street Journal* ran a headline: "The Failed Experiment of Covid Lockdowns. New data suggest that social distancing and reopening haven't determined the spread."[12] We can never improve on the Biblical solutions.

February 6, 2020 — Trump confirmed that a US airstrike in Yemen terminated Qasim al-Rimi, a founder and leader of al Qaeda in the Arabian Peninsula and deputy to al Qaeda leader Ayman al-Zawahiri.

GENESIS 12:3

I will bless those who bless you, And I will curse him who curses you...

EXODUS 23:22 (NET)

But if you diligently obey him and do all that I command, then I will be an enemy to your enemies, and I will be an adversary to your adversaries.

February 27, 2020 — Trump named Vice President Mike Pence to lead America's coronavirus response.

I believe this was not only because Trump saw the integrity of Mike Pence as vital, but God saw Pence as sanctified in the fight against a plague.

February 29, 2020 — Trump expanded travel restrictions against Iran due to their coronavirus epidemic[13], specifically no travel to Iran and no entry into the US by foreign nations who visited Iran in the last 14 days. Trump raised the travel advisory for South Korea and Italy to Level 4. The Food and Drug Administration (FDA) allowed certified labs to develop and test new coronavirus testing kits.

March 3, 2020 — CDC lifted federal restrictions on

coronavirus testing. Anyone can be tested for coronavirus subject to doctor's orders.

March 3, 2020 — President Trump donated his fourth-quarter salary to fight coronavirus.

March 6, 2020 — President Trump signed a coronavirus spending bill worth $8.3 billion.

March 9, 2020 — President Trump called on Congress to provide immediate payroll tax relief to citizens due to coronavirus business shutdowns.

March 10, 2020 — President Trump and VP Pence met with top health insurance companies and secured their commitment to waive co-pays for coronavirus testing.

March 11, 2020 — President Trump announced the suspension of travel from Europe for 30 days, excluding the UK and Ireland.

March 14, 2020 — President Trump announced the "European travel ban" will extend to the UK and Ireland.

March 18, 2020 — President Trump announced a temporary closure of the US-Canada border to non-essential traffic.

March 19, 2020 — President Trump announced promising news of an affordable drug that works against coronavirus when taken early: an arthritis drug that prevents malaria called Hydroxychloroquine.

March 20, 2020 — President Trump approved the first "major disaster declaration" for New York, the first and deadliest hotspot of coronavirus. A major disaster declaration is one step above an emergency declaration. Both allow public officials to exercise emergency powers (such as ordering an evacuation or stay-at-home lockdown), but the more extreme declaration means that local and state authorities can no longer cope with a disaster and are seeking long-term recovery assistance from the Federal Government.

March 22, 2020 — President Trump approved the second

and third disaster declarations for Washington and California, the early hotspots of the virus.

April 11, 2020 — All 50 states came under a major disaster declaration for the first time in US history, after President Trump approved Wyoming's declaration. It took 22 days[14] from the first declaration to the fiftieth.

April 13, 2020 — President Trump tweeted: "*For the first time in history there is a fully signed Presidential Disaster Declaration for all 50 States. We are winning, and will win, the war on the Invisible Enemy!*"

EXODUS 23:25 (NIV)

Worship the Lord your God, and his blessing will be on your food and water. I will take away sickness from among you,

April 15, 2020 — President Trump stopped funding the World Health Organization due to their misinformation about China's role in the pandemic and demanded "full accountability" over the Covid-19 pandemic.

PRESIDENT: "*Today I'm instructing my administration to halt funding of the World Health Organization while a review is conducted to assess the... organization's role in severely mismanaging and covering up the spread of the coronavirus... The WHO failed to investigate credible reports from sources in Wuhan that conflicted directly with the Chinese government's official accounts.*"[15]

This withdrawal of US contribution, to the tune of $400-$500 million per year, was a huge blow to the globalist agenda. The WHO is one of the unelected international bodies led by Marxist socialists like Director-General Tedros Adhanom Ghebreyesus. He publicly praised China in January and February 2020, even though China lied to the world, claiming coronavirus could not be spread from person to person. He publicly recommended that travel bans on China were unnecessary.

Taiwan should serve as a model for other nations: it effectively contained both H1N1 and coronavirus by quarantining the sick and without an economic lockdown. But the WHO refused to acknowledge Taiwan's success or its existence. When asked to comment on Taiwan by Hong Kong TV producer Yvonne Tong, the WHO Senior Advisor to the Director-General, a man named Dr. Bruce Aylward, simply hung up the Skype call. When the producer called him back, he said he couldn't hear her question, but she didn't need to ask again—just move on to the next question.[16] This kind of unscientific, politically-driven bias for China prompted President Trump to demand accountability from the WHO. No other politician had dared to question the WHO.

Globalists have long sought to control independent nations. A health scare was the perfect opportunity for them to push their radical agendas such as prolonged shutdowns of capitalist economies, mandatory masks, and mandatory vaccines, while protecting the origin of the virus—communist China. Trump had enough of it and hit them where it hurt—in their pockets.

China immediately pledged to contribute whatever the US would not give to the WHO. Interestingly, the WHO's second-biggest donor is not a nation, but Microsoft founder Bill Gates, a man who ironically is responsible for creating Outlook, a program whose early flaws led to the first computer viruses in 1999 (*Happy99*, *Melissa worm*, and *Kak worm*).[17] Gates has donated over $1.5 billion to the WHO. His top grant recipient "Gavi, the Vaccine Alliance" has received over $3.15 billion.[18]

REVELATION 6:2 (NKJ)

And I looked, and behold, a white horse. He who sat on it had a bow; and a crown was given to him, and he went out conquering and to conquer.

The first seal of the Book of Revelation is a white horse that had a bow (no arrows) and a crown with which he went out to conquer the world. The word "crown" in Latin is "corona." The only authorities whose advice has been able to shut down the world's travel and economies for the first time in human history are medical doctors who make official appearances in white coats. Therefore, it is possible that the White Horse of Revelation refers to the medical tyranny or "health dictatorship"[19] that is conquering the world without a bow or bullet. They are doing it by inflating the number of deaths from the "crown" virus from Wuhan, China.

End time control and deception seem to start with medical policies to serve the "public health." I do not doubt that quarantining the sick is necessary in a pandemic. But if "public health" were the primary drive of lockdown policy, why not keep people locked down until 99% of people quit smoking, stop sneezing, or drive at 10 mph?

Clearly, human freedom and rights are not to be infringed even at some cost to public health. Politicians should be honest about why they want to shut down schools (even though young, healthy people have virtually no risk of dying from COVID) and extend the economic lockdown. Fear makes people vote for change. Some journalists and Attorney General William Barr have suggested that the lockdown serves the Democrats' agenda because it encourages mail-in voting, which is subject to fraud, dead people voting, duplicate votes from residents who've lived in multiple states, as well as the increased likelihood of other countries tampering with the voting process..[20] They flatter us when they say "staying apart keeps us together."[21] We are to believe it's all for our good, not theirs.

DANIEL 11:21 (ESV)

And in his place shall stand up a contemptible person, to whom they had not given the honour of the kingdom:

but he shall come in time of security, and shall obtain the kingdom by flatteries.

April 30, 2020 — President Trump revealed a new initiative to combat the coronavirus epidemic through "Operation Warp Speed," described by the White House as "... a groundbreaking partnership between the Federal Government, scientific community, and private sector to develop and deliver vaccines in record time."[22]

ScienceMag explains that this project will select "vaccine candidates and pour essentially limitless resources into unprecedented comparative studies in animals, fast-tracked human trials, and manufacturing. Eschewing international cooperation—and any vaccine candidates from China—it hopes to have 300 million doses by January 2021 of a proven product, reserved for Americans."[23]

2 CHRONICLES 7:13-14

13 When I shut up heaven and there is no rain, or command the locusts to devour the land, or send PESTILENCE [plague or epidemic] **among My people,**

14 if My people who are called by My name will humble themselves, and pray and seek My face, and turn from their wicked ways, then I will hear from heaven, and will FORGIVE their sin and HEAL their land.

May 28, 2020 — President Trump issued an Executive Order on Preventing Online Censorship.

THE PRESIDENT: *"We're here today to defend free speech from one of the gravest dangers it has faced in American history, frankly... A small handful of powerful social media monopolies controls a vast portion of all public and private communications in the United States... They've had unchecked power to censor, restrict, edit, shape, hide, alter virtually any form of communication between private citizens and large public audiences. There's no precedent in American history for so small a number of corporations to control so large a sphere of human interaction...*

"The choices that Twitter makes when it chooses to suppress, edit, blacklist, shadow, ban are editorial decisions, pure and simple. They're editorial decisions. In those moments, Twitter ceases to be a neutral public platform, and they become an editor with a viewpoint. And I think we can say that about others also, whether you're looking at Google, whether you're looking at Facebook and perhaps others.

"One egregious example is when they try to silence views that they disagree with by selectively applying a 'fact check'... What they choose to fact check and what they choose to ignore or even promote is nothing more than a political activism group or political activism. And it's inappropriate...

"This censorship and bias is a threat to freedom itself. Imagine if your phone company silenced or edited your conversation. Social media companies have vastly more power and more reach than any phone company in the United States...

"My executive order further instructs the Federal Trade Commission, FTC, to prohibit social media companies from engaging in any deceptive acts or practices affecting commerce.

"... what they're doing is tantamount to monopoly, you can say. It's tantamount to taking over the airwaves. Can't let it happen. Otherwise, we're not going to have a democracy."[24]

This speech was reminiscent of JFK's address before the American Newspaper Publishers Association on April 27, 1961, in which he spoke against censorship and for transparency.

JFK: *"Without debate, without criticism, no Administration and no country can succeed—and no republic can survive. That is why the Athenian lawmaker Solon decreed it a crime for any citizen to shrink from controversy. And that is why our press was protected by the First Amendment—the only business in America specifically protected by the Constitution—not primarily to amuse and entertain, not to emphasize the trivial and the sentimental, not to simply 'give the public what it wants'—but to inform, to arouse, to reflect, to state our dangers and our opportunities, to indicate our crises and our choices, to lead, mold, educate and sometimes even anger public opinion.*

"This means greater coverage and analysis of international news —for it is no longer far away and foreign but close at hand and local. It means greater attention to improved understanding of the news as well as improved transmission. And it means, finally, that government at all levels must meet its obligation to provide you with the fullest possible information outside the narrowest limits of national security—and we intend to do it."[25]

We have little responsible press today, as evidenced by:

1) The unmitigated lies of corporate media, such as

a) reporting that Trump had 0-1% chance of winning the 2016 election;

b) peddling the Russian Collusion hoax for three years after;

c) maligning the reputation of Justice Brett Kavanaugh and believing a false allegation because it came from a Democrat psychologist;

d) reporting Jussie Smollett's fake hate crime allegation without the shallowest investigation);

e) speculating that Trump may have Parkinson's because he drank a glass of water with two hands; and

2) The blatant censorship of conservative voices, such as:

a) Apple, Facebook, Spotify, and YouTube de-platforming Alex Jones simultaneously on August 5, 2018 (I call it the day freedom of speech died);

b) Paypal banning Bitchute (an alternative to YouTube) in November 2018, and Patreon deactivating the fundraising accounts of Milo Yiannopoulos (a gay conservative) and Carl Benjamin (Sargon of Akkad on Youtube) in December 2018;

c) YouTube deplatforming Stefan Molyneux, unsubscribing

his 1 million followers and erasing thousands of his videos on June 29, 2020;

d) YouTube and Twitter's deleting links to the April 2020 viral video of two medical doctors in Bakersfield, Dr. Dan Erickson and Dr. Artin Massihi, urging an end to lockdowns;[26] and

e) Facebook, Twitter, and YouTube's removing links to the August 2020 viral video of a dozen doctors from America's Frontline Doctors, standing on the steps of the US Capitol, promoting Hydroxychloroquine as part of effective, early treatment of COVID19, and discussing the negative impacts of the shutdown orders in terms of mental illness, family violence, suicide and substance abuse problems.

If you search for the video now, Google will not give you any results for the video. It's a blackout. It has been less than a month since the doctors spoke in Washington, DC, till the writing of this book. It is a frightening level of information control.[27]

Not only is there online censorship, but the nature of the bias behind the censorship can be buried by algorithms that virtually no politician understands. Algorithms are not magic; they are a series of instructions written by humans who tell the computers what to do, not vice versa. Computers do not decide for themselves what information is truth or what news is "intolerant," "divisive," or "hateful." Humans program their biases into a set of instructions called algorithms.

Social media is described in this psalm.

Psalm 37:12 (ESV)

The wicked plots against the righteous and gnashes his teeth at him,

Despite the censorship, the Lord promises that the truth will prevail.

Isaiah 51:7 (ESV)

"Listen to me, you who know righteousness, the people in whose heart is my law; fear not the reproach of man, nor be dismayed at their revilings."

My proposals for a Digital Bill of Rights, which will protect users' private data, disempower corporate media, and level the playing field of social media are in my book *Trump's Unfinished Business,* chapter 4, "Digital Bill of Rights, Big Tech & Fake News."[28]

June 2, 2020 — President Trump issued an Executive Order on Advancing International Religious Freedom. This order prioritized international religious freedom and integrated concerns of religious persecution as a factor in US diplomacy.

THE PRESIDENT: *"As stated in the 2017 National Security Strategy, our Founders understood religious freedom not as a creation of the state, but as a gift of God to every person and a right that is fundamental for the flourishing of our society...*

"Within 180 days of the date of this order, the Secretary of State (Secretary) shall, in consultation with the Administrator of the United States Agency for International Development (USAID), develop a plan to prioritize international religious freedom in the planning and implementation of United States foreign policy and in the foreign assistance programs of the Department of State and USAID...

"The Secretary shall direct Chiefs of Mission in countries of particular concern, countries on the Special Watch List, countries in which there are entities of particular concern, and any other countries that have engaged in or tolerated violations of religious freedom... to develop comprehensive action plans to... advance international religious freedom and to encourage the host governments to make progress in eliminating violations of religious freedom.

"In meetings with their counterparts in foreign governments, the

heads of agencies shall, when appropriate and in coordination with the Secretary, raise concerns about international religious freedom and cases that involve individuals imprisoned because of their religion."[29]

PROVERBS 28:5 (ESV)

Evil men do not understand justice, but those who seek the Lord understand it completely.

MATTHEW 5:10

Blessed are those who are persecuted for righteousness' sake, For theirs is the kingdom of heaven.

June 21, 2020 — President Trump held his first public rally since the coronavirus lockdown. The Tulsa Rally was an achievement in at least two ways:

1. the leader of the free world was out in public without a mask—it made people feel normal—they longed for social interaction and outdoor events to be restored;[30]
2. it was a speech most akin to JFK's famous 1961 speech exposing the Deep State and calling on Americans, including the free press, to fight against globalists. Trump addressed the elites, even mocked them, and did it with humor.

THE PRESIDENT:

On Religious Liberty: *"They want to crush religious liberty, they don't want religion. Silence religious believers, indoctrinate your children with hateful and vicious lies about our country, subsidize late-term abortion and afterbirth execution. They want to punish your thought but not their violent crimes."*

On the Riots: *"20 of 20 of the most dangerous cities in America* *are controlled by Democrats. Think of that, 20 of 20, and so is nearly every major city. The murder rate in Baltimore and Detroit is higher than El Salvador, Guatemala, or even Afghanistan."*

On Globalists and the Military Industrial Complex: *"When I get foreign nations to pay us billions and billions of dollars, nobody wants to talk about that. When I take soldiers out of countries because they're not treating us properly, Germany is an example. I mean I have a German heritage like some of you. I said, 'Let's get it down from 50,000 to 25,000 because they're delinquent. For many years they're delinquent. They haven't been paying what they're supposed to be paying. They're paying 1% instead of 2% and 2% is a very low number,' and they say, 'Yes, we think by 2030, maybe 2032, we could get current.' I said, 'No, Angela [Merkel], please. Don't say that, Angela.' It's true. You know who I'm talking about. By the way, very nice woman. Very good negotiator. I said, 'Angela, that's a long time,' this was in 2019. She said 2032. I said, 'No, Angela, that's not working...' But I said. 'Well, what about the last 25 years? All the money you owe us?' Everybody forgot about that. They forget about all the money that wasn't paid. I said, 'What about the trillion dollars that you really owe?' So we're negotiating, let's see, but in the meantime, we're reducing our troops.*

"Remember this: we're supposed to protect Germany from Russia, but Germany is paying Russia billions of dollars for energy coming from a brand new pipeline. So they pay the country we're supposed to protect them from—they pay billions of dollars to that country. We're supposed to protect them. Excuse me, how does that work?

"... We cannot continue to be ripped off. We're ripped off by so many countries and we're stopping it. And ***that means that a lot of people don't want me here.*** *They don't want me. There are a lot of people that don't want me. They don't sell a lot of bombs when we're not dropping bombs on people. You know that, right? It's called* ***the military industrial complex****."*

This unusually frank account of a private, political exchange with the most powerful woman in the European

Union, Angela Merkel, was reminiscent of JFK's speech which may have caused him to get assassinated 940 days later.

JFK (April 27, 1961): *"The very word 'secrecy' is repugnant in a free and open society; and we are as a people inherently and historically opposed to secret societies, to secret oaths and to secret proceedings. We decided long ago that the dangers of excessive and unwarranted concealment of pertinent facts far outweighed the dangers which are cited to justify it. Even today, there is little value in opposing the threat of a closed society by imitating its arbitrary restrictions. Even today, there is little value in insuring the survival of our nation if our traditions do not survive with it. And there is very grave danger that an announced need for increased security will be seized upon by those anxious to expand its meaning to the very limits of official censorship and concealment.*

"Today no war has been declared—and however fierce the struggle may be, it may never be declared in the traditional fashion. Our way of life is under attack. Those who make themselves our enemy are advancing around the globe. The survival of our friends is in danger. And yet no war has been declared, no borders have been crossed by marching troops, no missiles have been fired.

"If the press is awaiting a declaration of war before it imposes the self-discipline of combat conditions, then I can only say that no war ever posed a greater threat to our security. If you are awaiting a finding of 'clear and present danger,' then I can only say that the danger has never been more clear and its presence has never been more imminent... For we are opposed around the world by a monolithic and ruthless conspiracy... Its preparations are concealed, not published. Its mistakes are buried, not headlined. Its dissenters are silenced, not praised. No expenditure is questioned, no rumor is printed, no secret is revealed."[31]

PSALM 25:19 (ESV)

Consider how many are my foes, and with what violent hatred they hate me.

PRESIDENT TRUMP continued outlining the collectivist, globalist agenda of Joe Biden:

"Joe Biden and the Democrats want to prosecute Americans for going to church, but not for burning a church. They believe you can riot, vandalize and destroy, but you cannot attend a peaceful pro-America rally. They want to punish your thought, but not their violent crimes...

"When the chips are down, Biden will always cave to the radical left... Joe Biden will always let you down. That's been his history. At my direction early this year, the heroes of the US military took out the world's top terrorist, the savage killer leader of ISIS al-Baghdadi and the number one terrorist, anywhere in the world, Qasem Soleimani. We took them out. Joe Biden opposed killing Soleimani... We killed this number one terrorist. He didn't like it. You know why he didn't like it? Because he thought it would be good politically—that didn't work out too well. Just as he opposed the raid that killed Osama bin Laden. He opposed it—you know that.

"Biden is always on the wrong side of history, as said by people that are with him and worked with him. He never made a correct foreign policy decision. Biden is a puppet for China. Son walked out with 1.5 billion... Allowing them to rip off America for many years. Now they're paying us billions and billions of dollars. We give a lot of it to our farmers. We have plenty left over. China is not exactly happy with me. They pay us billions and billions of dollars."

On the Elites: *"Somebody two days ago said, 'Sir, the elite are really working hard on trying to destroy you.' I said, 'Yeah, why do you call them the elite,' I said, 'why?' 'Well, they're not elite.' I look better than them. Much more handsome. Got better hair than they do. I got nicer properties. I got nicer houses. I got nicer apartments. I got nicer everything. I ran for politics once, just once in my life. And I became President of the United States..."*

On the Democrats' Agenda: *"Biden is a very willing Trojan horse for socialism... He hollowed out our middle class, including our black middle class with open borders. Trapped young children in failing government schools, built cages. Those cages were built by Obama and Biden. Look it up, 2014. And the fake news doesn't wanted to...*

"Virtually every policy that has hurt black Americans for half a century, Joe Biden has supported or enacted. I've done more for the black community in four years than Joe Biden has done in 47 years. Racial justice begins with Joe Biden's retirement from public life.

"... We will end deadly sanctuary cities. We will finish the wall, which has now 212 miles built and beautiful..."

Conclusion: *"We believe that faith and family, not government and bureaucracy, are the true American way. We believe that children should be taught to love our country, honor our history, and always salute our great American flag. And we live by the words of our national motto, it will never change, 'In God we trust.' We stand on the shoulders of American heroes who crossed the oceans, blazed the trails, settled the continent, tamed the wilderness, dug out the Panama Canal, laid down the railroads, revolutionized industries, won two world wars, defeated fascism and communism, and made America the single greatest nation in the history of the world. And we are making it greater and greater every single day."*[32]

PSALM 64:2 (NIV)

Hide me from the conspiracy of the wicked, from the plots of evildoers.

DEUTERONOMY 28:7 (NIV)

The Lord will grant that the enemies who rise up against you will be defeated before you. They will come at you from one direction but flee from you in seven.

June 26, 2020 — President Trump issued an Executive Order on Protecting American Monuments, Memorials, and Statues and Combating Recent Criminal Violence.

Context: On May 25, a black American died while being

arrested by police in Minneapolis, Minnesota. Before we saw the footage from the police body camera (leaked on August 3rd) and the toxicology report of George Floyd's blood, protesters assumed Floyd died of police brutality and began to riot, loot and set fire to businesses in violation to the coronavirus lockdown.

Democrats not only chose to appease the rioters, but many encouraged them by posting bail for them if they got arrested. After a month, the rioters bizarrely began targeting historical statues, even of Christian abolitionists, civil rights leaders and the European discoverer of the American continent, Christopher Columbus. The riots no longer had anything to do with George Floyd. It was anarchy for political gain—to ruin Trump's chances of reelection. Victims lost their livelihoods—some lost their lives—in the increasingly senseless violence.

Trump put a stop to it with an executive order that imposed a 10-year jail sentence on anyone caught defacing or destroying federal property.

THE PRESIDENT: *"The first duty of government is to ensure domestic tranquility and defend the life, property, and rights of its citizens. Over the last 5 weeks, there has been a sustained assault on the life and property of civilians, law enforcement officers, government property, and revered American monuments such as the Lincoln Memorial. Many of the rioters, arsonists, and left-wing extremists who have carried out and supported these acts have explicitly identified themselves with ideologies—such as Marxism—that call for the destruction of the United States system of government.*

"Anarchists and left-wing extremists have sought to advance a fringe ideology that paints the United States of America as fundamentally unjust and have sought to impose that ideology on Americans through violence and mob intimidation. They have led riots in the streets, burned police vehicles, killed and assaulted government officers as well as business owners defending their

property, and even seized an area within one city where law and order gave way to anarchy. During the unrest, innocent citizens also have been harmed and killed.

"... Individuals and organizations have the right to peacefully advocate for either the removal or the construction of any monument. But no individual or group has the right to damage, deface, or remove any monument by use of force.

"In the midst of these attacks, many State and local governments appear to have lost the ability to distinguish between the lawful exercise of rights to free speech and assembly and unvarnished vandalism. They have surrendered to mob rule... My Administration will not allow violent mobs incited by a radical fringe to become the arbiters of the aspects of our history that can be celebrated in public spaces."[33]

PROVERBS 22:28 (ESV)

Do not move the ancient landmark that your fathers have set.

July 1, 2020 — the United States-Mexico-Canada (USMCA) trade agreement went into effect, rendering obsolete the outdated NAFTA signed by Bill Clinton. This new trade arrangement is expected to add 600,000 jobs and grow US GDP by $235 billion.[34]

July 8, 2020 — the Supreme Court ruled in favor of religious freedom in *Little Sisters of the Poor v. Pennsylvania*. The case dealt with Obama's Affordable Care Act's contraception mandate, which obliged employers to provide cost-free coverage for contraceptives, sterilizations, and "emergency birth control" in employee health plans, regardless of religious or moral objections.

HSS SECRETARY ALEX AZAR: *"Today's ruling is a major victory for President Trump's defense of religious liberty and protects Americans of faith who provide vital healthcare and social services to millions of Americans, especially the needy and vulnerable. It is a shame that nuns ever had to go to the Supreme Court to ensure they can care for the elderly poor without violating their consciences, but thanks to their courageous advocacy and the leadership of President Trump, they–and all Americans of faith–have now triumphed... The Trump Administration took action to vindicate the rights of religious and moral people to be free from unnecessary government burdens, and the court has upheld the Administration's action."*[35]

> **GALATIANS 4:16 (ESV)**
>
> **Have I then become your enemy by telling you the truth.**

> **ACTS 4:19-20 (ESV)**
>
> **But Peter and John answered them, "Whether it is right in the sight of God to listen to you rather than to God, you must judge, for we cannot but speak of what we have seen and heard."**

July 27, 2020 — President Trump took on the pharmaceutical industry and signed four executive orders to reduce prescription drug prices. For decades Americans paid higher prices for prescription drugs than other developed countries—an estimated 80% more. Congress refused to act against the interest of powerful lobbyists for Big Pharma.

THE PRESIDENT: *"The four orders that I'm signing today will completely restructure the prescription drug market, in terms of pricing and everything else, to make these medications affordable and accessible for all Americans."*[36]

1. The first order directs federally qualified health centers to pass along massive discounts on insulin and epinephrine from drug companies to low-income Americans.

2. The second order will allow the safe, legal importation of

prescription drugs from Canada and other countries where the price for identical drugs is lower.

3. The third order will prohibit secret deals between drug manufacturers and pharmacy middlemen (called "benefit managers"), ensuring patients directly benefit from discounts.

4. The fourth order ensures the United States gets "favored nation" status by paying the lowest price available among economically advanced countries for Medicare Part B drugs.

These acts created many more enemies for President Trump. He needs our prayers.

REVELATION 18:23

...For your merchants were the great men of the earth, for by your sorcery [Greek: pharmakeia] **all the nations were deceived.**

In the Bible, the word for "pharmacy" is the same as "sorcery." It is an odd cognate until you realize that both drugs and sorcery create a dependent class—people who rely on a force they do not understand to get the feelings they need. Freedom is lost when we give ourselves to sorcery or drug companies.

ROMANS 6:16 (NLT)

Don't you realize that you become the slave of whatever you choose to obey?

August 5, 2020 — Vice President Mike Pence becomes the first vice president to visit a pregnancy resource center, which offers abortion-free pregnancy services for women. He then spoke at the Starkey Road Baptist Church in Seminole, Florida, calling President Trump "the most pro-life President in American history."

THE VICE PRESIDENT: *"From the first day he took office,*

President Trump has been standing without apology for the sanctity of human life... President Trump became the first President in American history to address the March for Life in person on the National Mall... So life is winning in America... I believe with all my heart that the men and women of the pro-life movement do not fight alone. He who said, 'Before I formed you in the womb, I knew you,' fights with you."[37]

August 6, 2020 — President Trump signed an executive order to expand "Made in America" production, establish "Made in America" rules for Federal Government agencies, and bring manufacturing jobs back to America. Speaking to workers at a Whirlpool manufacturing plant in Clyde, Ohio, the President stated:

"Globalization has made the financial elites who donate to politicians very wealthy, but it's left millions and millions of our workers with nothing but poverty and heartache—and our towns and cities with empty factories and plants.

"We're fighting for Main Street, not Wall Street. We have rejected globalism and embraced patriotism."[38]

THE WHITE HOUSE: *"As a result, his list of trade accomplishments keeps growing. NAFTA is gone, replaced by a far stronger United States-Mexico-Canada Agreement. China and its enablers on the global stage are at last being held accountable. Trade agreements with South Korea, Japan, and others have been renegotiated to protect American jobs and customers."*[39]

August 13, 2020 — President Trump announced the Abraham Accord, a Peace Agreement between Israel and the United Arab Emirates (UAE).

Bible prophecy predicts that there must be a time of peace and prosperity in the Middle East before the anti-Christ will arise and "confirm a covenant with many for one week (a Hebraic unit of any seven, in this context a 'week of 7 years')."

Some Christians are scared of peace treaties, but we should not be. Peace treaties end conflict and war. Jesus said, "Blessed are the peacemakers, for they shall be called sons of God" (Matthew 5:9 NKJV).

Contrary to many eschatological assumptions, the Bible does not say the anti-Christ is going to sign a new peace treaty. Instead, he will "confirm the covenant" as the Douay-Rheims Bible translates Daniel 9:27, a prediction that is 2,500 years old.

Which covenant is God referring to? The most logical choice is the most obvious one: the only covenant that has been contested for 4,000 years—the covenant the Lord made with Abraham to give his children the Promise Land.

GENESIS 15:18

On the same day the Lord made a covenant with Abram, saying: "To your descendants I have given this land, from the river of Egypt to the great river, the River Euphrates"—

The Jews are the only people on earth who have a 4,000-year-old written title deed to their land. Nobody else can claim this certain possession of the land they're living on. Yet the Jews' right to exist on their land is constantly vilified and threatened by its neighbors, especially their closest neighbors the Arab Palestinians.

When I stood on the Aqaba side of the Jordanian-Saudi Arabian border in May 2017, the Spirit of the Lord showed me that Trump would take the negotiation cards away from the Palestinians. Because Trump is an accomplished negotiator, he by nature is looking for a deal.

Politicians reached a stalemate because they couldn't get the Palestinians to make a deal that includes recognizing Israel's covenant with God and with their land. Since Israel's rebirth in 1948, no Western politician could resolve this. Every ceasefire eventually got violated. Even the "historic" Oslo Peace Accord of 1993 was broken. Obama in 8 years could not resolve the conflict in the Middle East and said "you can't fix everything.[40]"

Pundits did not believe Trump would be any different than his predecessors. I felt differently. My premonition was that the President was not going to act like a politician. He was going to do something unprecedented in the Middle East. I predicted that if the Palestinians wouldn't make a deal with him, he would go find another party to make a deal with (Saudi Arabia was on my mind as I looked across the horizon into the desert kingdom). Any deal with another Arab state would isolate the Palestinian National Authority and may cause them to regret being left out of great regional deals.

The Abraham Accord is a great deal for both sides, symbolically and tangibly. Dubai, the largest city in the UAE, is the leading financial center of the Middle East and is a hub for air traffic and tourism. Israel offers technology, commerce and military cooperation. Symbolically, Israel would like Arabs to know, contrary to misinformation they are fed, that they can come to worship freely, without harassment, in Jerusalem and on the Temple Mount.

Both Ezekiel and Revelation indicate that Israel and the Middle East will be in a time of peace and prosperity before the anti-Christ arises and "sudden destruction" comes. The normalization of relations between Arab nations and Israel is to be seen as part of the path to prophecy fulfillment, and peace in itself is a good thing for the Gospel. When Arab nations allow Israelis the freedoms to travel, do business and worship without persecution in Arab nations, opportunities to share the Gospel will multiply.

This is, in fact, why we pray "for kings and all who are in authority, that we may lead a quiet and peaceable life in all godliness and reverence. For this is good and acceptable in the sight of God our Savior, who desires all men to be saved and to come to the knowledge of the truth" (1 Timothy 2:2-4). People go to church and get saved in times of peace. People live in fear, flee for their lives, or get imprisoned during times of war.

The conditions before Armageddon is one of regional peace and prosperity.

EZEKIEL 38:11

You [Gog, the leader of an invading force including the armies of Turkey, Iran, Libya and Sudan] will say, "I will go up against a land of unwalled villages; I will go to a PEACEFUL people, who dwell SAFELY, all of them dwelling WITHOUT WALLS, and having neither bars nor gates"—to take plunder and to take booty...

Listen to the world's response when Babylon (the ancient empire stretching from Iraq to Saudi Arabia) is destroyed in one day. People mourned for New York because it is the financial center of America and a big tourist attraction. People don't mourn for Inner Mongolia because most people haven't been there. At the time of this writing, I have not been to Saudi Arabia yet and only know three people who have been there. This is about to change.

REVELATION 18:11-12, 17-19

11 And the merchants of the earth will weep and mourn over her, for no one buys their merchandise anymore:

12 merchandise of gold and silver, precious stones and pearls, fine linen and purple, silk and scarlet, every kind of citron wood...

17 For in one hour such great riches came to nothing. Every shipmaster, all who travel by ship, sailors, and as many as trade on the sea, stood at a distance

18 and cried out when they saw the smoke of her burning, saying, "What is like this great city?"

19 They threw dust on their heads and cried out,

weeping and wailing, and saying, "Alas, alas, that great city, in which all who had ships on the sea became rich by her wealth! For in one hour she is made desolate."

The peace Trump is negotiating is good. It will bring years of prosperity and increased opportunities for the Gospel.

Of course, no peace on earth lasts forever. One day the citizens of Israel will be lulled into a false sense of security and peace. Rather than thanking God for a Christian President who followed the Bible and helped broker peace, Israelis will become more secular, more antagonistic to the Name Jesus, and more proud of their defense force (IDF). That is when they will be betrayed by an anti-Christ figure who "confirms the covenant" for seven years, only to break his word halfway into the period.

This betrayal will last a maximum of three and a half years. We are not living for the worst days to come. We are living for the best days ahead. We are pursuing peace for the sake of the Gospel to be heard.

The Holy Spirit said, "If it is possible, as much as depends on you, live peaceably with all men" (Romans 12:18 NKJV).

August 24, 2020 — President Trump invited 6 former hostages to the Oval Office whom his Administration helped set free.

THE PRESIDENT: "We have 6 incredible people who were held hostage by various countries and I am very pleased to let everybody know that we brought back over 50 hostages from 22 different countries. We worked very hard on it."[41]

Among them were Pastor Andrew Brunson, arrested in Turkey in the aftermath of a failed 2016 coup, and Michael White, a US Navy veteran arrested in Iran in 2018 while visiting a girlfriend he had met online. White was sentenced to 13 years in prison for insulting the country's top leader. He was released after 683 days in captivity.[42]

GALATIANS 6:2 (NET)

Carry one another's burdens, and in this way you will fulfill the law of Christ.

Why is Trump so successful in getting hostages home? Joel Simon wrote on February 20, 2020 about Trump's off-script departure from the foreign policy of his predecessors. Since 1973, when Nixon refused to negotiate with terrorists and two American diplomats were shot by Palestinian terrorists, America's policy has been "we don't negotiate with terrorists." Simon wrote in *The NewYorker*:

"President Trump has taken a very different approach to the issue...Trump's style of resolving cases is more personal and more flexible. Obama was focussed on the strategic challenges around hostage-taking, and tended to avoid personal interest or involvement. If an American President showed a personal interest in bringing a hostage home, the theory went, it would raise the value of American hostages and increase the number of kidnappings. Trump, by contrast, has gone out of his way to highlight his personal engagement in hostage-recovery efforts, welcoming hostages home on national television or inviting them to Oval Office photo opportunities... Peter Bergen, a vice-president of the Washington, D.C.-based New America think tank who has written widely on terrorism, called Trump's hostage efforts 'an area of significant foreign-policy success'..."[43]

One of the ways to be able to negotiate with people who may have malintent is to trust God to take vengeance on those who take advantage of you. This allows you to negotiate from a place of freedom and peace.

1 CHRONICLES 12:17

And David went out to meet them [soldiers of the tribes of Benjamin and Judah], **and answered and said to them, "If**

> **you have come peaceably to me to help me, my heart will be united with you; but if to betray me to my enemies, since there is no wrong in my hands, may the God of our fathers look and bring judgment."**

August 24, 2020 — The First Day of the Republican National Convention (RNC), held the week following the Democratic National Convention (DNC). Both were the first time conventions were held online due to coronavirus restrictions.

I include what I consider the best speech of the first day mainly because it illustrates how much the President has been able to accomplish despite being constantly under attack.

Herschel Walker, an African America football star, winner of the 1982 Heisman Trophy and College Football Hall of Famer in 1999, gave a powerful 3-minute speech:

"Most of you know me as a football player, but I'm also a father, a man of faith, and a very good judge of character. I've known Donald Trump for 37 years. I don't mean just casual ran into him from time to time. I'm talking about a deep personal friendship...

"It hurts my soul to hear the terrible names that people call Donald. The worst one is 'racist.' I take it as a personal insult that people would think I've had a 37-year friendship with a racist!

"People who think that don't know what they're talking about. Growing up in the deep South, I've seen racism up close. I know what it is and it isn't Donald Trump.

"... He shows how much he cares about social justice in the black community through his actions and his actions speaks louder than stickers or slogans on a jersey. He keeps right on fighting to improve the lives of black Americans and all Americans. He works night and day. He never stops. He leaves nothing on the field. Some people don't like his style, the way he knocks down obstacles that get in the way of his goals. People on the opposing team they don't like when I ran over them either, but that's how you get the job done.

"I pray every night that God gives him more time, give him four more years. He has accomplished so much almost all by himself on a constant attack, but there's still more work to be done. If you love America and want to make it better, Donald Trump is your president. He's my president and I'm blessed to call him friend."[44]

August 26, 2020 — The Third Day of the RNC. I include what I consider the best speech of the third day. It was from a black American Democrat who believe in Jesus! Such defectors are the Left's worst nightmare.

Jack Brewer spoke boldly for God, *"I'm Jack Brewer, a former three-time NFL team captain, college professor, coach, husband, son, and father. I'm also a lifelong Democrat, but I support Donald Trump. Let me be clear, I didn't come here for the popularity or the praise, the likes or the retweets, I'm here as a servant to God, a servant to the people of our nation and a servant to our president...*

"I'm fed up with the way he's portrayed in the media, who refuse to acknowledge what he's actually done for the black community. It's confusing the minds of our innocent children. Before I left to come deliver this message, my energetic eight year old son, Jackson, stopped me and said, "Dad, can you please just tell everyone that all lives need to matter and that God loves everyone?"

In that moment, I realized that my eight year old had figured out what so many adults have seemed to forget; we are not as divided as our politics suggest. At some point, for the sake of our children, the policies must take priority over the personalities. So because you have an issue with President Trump's tone, you're going to allow Biden and Harris to deny underserved black and brown children school of choice?

"Are we so offended by the president's campaign slogan—Make America Great Again—that we're going to ignore that Joe Biden and Kamala Harris have collectively been responsible for locking up countless black men for nonviolent crimes? Are you going to allow the media to lie to you by falsely claiming that he said there are very fine white supremacists in Charlottesville? He didn't say that, it's a lie.

And ignore the so-called 'Black Lives Matter' organization that openly, on their website, called for the destruction of the nuclear family? My fellow Americans, our families need each other. We need black fathers in the homes with their wives and children. The future of our communities depend on it. I'm blessed to be able to run inner city youth programs and to also teach in prisons across America. The inmates in my federal prison program literally receive days off their sentence just for attending my class.

"And that's thanks to President Donald Trump in his First Step Act... Our president has made incredible strides to end mass incarceration and give unprecedented opportunities for blacks in America to rise. America, let this election be a call for all God's people who are called by his name to humble ourselves and pray together, and to seek his face and to turn from our wicked ways. Then he will hear us from heaven and he will forgive our sins and he will heal our land. Amen, and God bless America."[45]

August 27, 2020 — Alice Johnson, whose life sentence was commuted by the President on June 6, 2018, made the following Christian speech on the last day of the Republican National Convention:

"Some say, 'You do the crime. You do the time.' However, that time should be fair and just. We've all made mistakes, and none of us want to be defined forever based on our worst decision. While in prison, I became a playwright, a mentor, a certified hospice volunteer, an ordained minister, and received the Special Olympics Event Coordinator of the year award for my work with disabled women. Because the only thing worse than unjustly imprisoning my body is trying to imprison my mind.

"When President Trump heard about me—about the injustice of my story—he saw me as a person. He had compassion. And he acted. Free in body thanks to President Trump. But free in mind thanks to the Almighty God. I couldn't believe it. I always remembered that God knew my name, even in my darkest hour. But I never thought a President would.

"Six months after President Trump granted me a second chance, he signed the First Step Act into law. It was REAL justice reform. And it brought joy, hope, and freedom to thousands of well-deserving people. I hollered Hallelujah! My faith in justice and mercy was rewarded."[46]

I believe we Christians can join in a chorus of "Hallelujah!" with Sister Johnson: Justice is coming!

PSALM 118:5 (ESV)

Out of my distress I called on the Lord; the Lord answered me and set me free.

PHILEMON 1:11 (NIV)

Formerly he [Onesimus] **was useless to you** [Philemon] **but now he has become useful both to you and to me.**

August 28, 2020 — President Trump's acceptance speech of his party's nomination for President is his last speech to be included in this list of accomplishments. It summarized his commitment to defend America against Christian bigotry and marxist globalism.

THE PRESIDENT: *"My fellow Americans, tonight, with a heart full of gratitude and boundless optimism, I proudly accept this nomination for President of the United States...*

"In the left's backward view, they do not see America as the most free, just, and exceptional nation on earth. Instead, they see a wicked nation that must be punished for its sins.

"Our opponents say that redemption for YOU can only come from giving power to THEM. This is a tired anthem spoken by every repressive movement throughout history.

"But in this country, we don't look to career politicians for salvation. In America, we don't turn to government to restore our souls—we put our faith in Almighty God.

"Joe Biden is not the savior of America's soul—he is the destroyer

of America's Jobs, and if given the chance, he will be the destroyer of American Greatness.

"For 47 years, Joe Biden took the donations of blue collar workers, gave them hugs and even kisses, and told them he felt their pain—and then he flew back to Washington and voted to ship their jobs to China and many other distant lands. Joe Biden spent his entire career outsourcing the dreams of American Workers, offshoring their jobs, opening their borders, and sending their sons and daughters to fight in endless foreign wars...

"From the moment I left my former life behind, and a good life it was, I have done nothing but fight for YOU. I did what our political establishment never expected and could never forgive, breaking the cardinal rule of Washington Politics. I KEPT MY PROMISES.

"Together, we have ended the rule of the failed political class—and they are desperate to get their power back by any means necessary. They are angry at me because instead of putting THEM FIRST, I put AMERICA FIRST!

"... Last month, I took on Big Pharma and signed orders that will massively lower the cost of your prescription drugs, and to give critically ill patients access to lifesaving cures, we passed the decades long-awaited RIGHT TO TRY legislation. We also passed VA Accountability and VA Choice...

"Unlike previous administrations, I have kept America OUT of new wars—and our troops are coming home. We have spent nearly $2.5 trillion on completely rebuilding our military, which was very badly depleted when I took office. This includes three separate pay raises for our great warriors.

"... China supports Joe Biden and desperately wants him to win. China would own our country if Joe Biden got elected. Unlike Biden, I will hold them fully accountable for the tragedy they caused. In recent months, our nation, and the rest of the world, has been hit with a once-in-a-century pandemic that China allowed to spread around the globe... We will also provide tax credits to bring jobs out of China BACK to America—and we will impose tariffs on any

company that leaves America to produce jobs overseas. We'll make sure our companies and jobs stay in our country, as I've already been doing.

"Joe Biden's agenda is Made in China. My agenda is MADE IN THE USA.

"Biden has promised to abolish the production of American oil, coal, shale, and natural gas—laying waste to the economies of Pennsylvania, Ohio, Texas, North Dakota, Oklahoma, Colorado, and New Mexico. Millions of jobs will be lost, and energy prices will soar. These same policies led to crippling power outages in California just last week. How can Joe Biden claim to be an "ally of the Light" when his own party can't even keep the lights on?

"... Biden also vowed to oppose School Choice and close down Charter Schools, ripping away the ladder of opportunity for Black and Hispanic children.

"In a second term, I will EXPAND charter schools and provide SCHOOL CHOICE to every family in America. And we will always treat our teachers with the tremendous respect they deserve.

"Joe Biden claims he has empathy for the vulnerable—yet the party he leads supports the extreme late-term abortion of defenseless babies right up to the moment of BIRTH. Democrat leaders talk about moral decency, but they have no problem with stopping a baby's beating heart in the 9th month of pregnancy.

"Democrat politicians refuse to protect innocent life, and then they lecture us about morality and saving America's soul? Tonight, we proudly declare that all children, born and unborn, have a GOD-GIVEN RIGHT TO LIFE.

"During the Democrat Convention, the words 'Under God' were removed from the Pledge of Allegiance—not once, but twice. The fact is, this is where they are coming from...

"Last year, over 1,000 African-Americans were murdered as result of violent crime in just four Democrat-run cities. The top 10 most dangerous cities in the country are run by Democrats, and have been for decades. Thousands more African-Americans are victims of

violent crime in these communities. Joe Biden and the left ignore these American Victims. I NEVER WILL.

"... We must reclaim our independence from the left's repressive mandates. Americans are exhausted trying to keep up with the latest list of approved words and phrases, and the ever-more restrictive political decrees. Many things have a different name now, and the rules are constantly changing. The goal of cancel culture is to make decent Americans live in fear of being fired, expelled, shamed, humiliated, and driven from society as we know it. The far-left wants to coerce you into saying what you know to be FALSE and scare you out of saying what you know to be TRUE.

"But on November 3rd, you can send them a thundering message they will never forget!

"... Our opponents believe that America is a depraved nation. We want our sons and daughters to know the truth: America is the greatest and most exceptional nation in the history of the world!

"Our country wasn't built by cancel culture, speech codes, and soul-crushing conformity. We are NOT a nation of timid spirits. We are a nation of fierce, proud, and independent American Patriots.

"We are a nation of pilgrims, pioneers, adventurers, explorers and trailblazers who refused to be tied down, held back, or reined in. Americans have steel in their spines, grit in their souls, and fire in their hearts. There is no one like us on earth."[47]

Stifling speech codes and intolerance to Christianity have met their match in the avenger, President Trump.

ACTS 5:29 (ESV)

But Peter and the apostles answered, "We must obey God rather than men.

September 4, 2020 — President Trump brokered an agreement between largely-Christian Serbia and mainly-Muslim Kosovo that included Kosovo recognizing Israel and Serbia agreeing to move its embassy to Jerusalem. Peace in the

Balkans and the Middle East should have been front page news, but one could have entirely missed this story buried in the back pages of world news.

THE PRESIDENT: *"Today, I am pleased to announce yet another historic commitment. Serbia and Kosovo have each committed to economic normalization. After a violent and tragic history and years of failed negotiations, my Administration proposed a new way of bridging the divide. By focusing on job creation and economic growth, the two countries were able to reach a real breakthrough on economic cooperation across a broad range of issues.*

"We have also made additional progress on reaching ***peace in the Middle East****. Kosovo and Israel have agreed to normalization of ties and the establishment of diplomatic relations. Serbia has committed to opening a commercial office in Jerusalem this month and to move its embassy to Jerusalem by July.*

"It has taken tremendous bravery by President Vučić of Serbia and Prime Minister Hoti of Kosovo to embark on these talks and to come to Washington to finalize these commitments. By doing so, they have made their countries, the Balkans, and the world safer."[48]

The European Union had mediated talks between the two countries for more than a decade without success. Serbia and Kosovo will not only normalize economic relations, but Serbia will follow the examples of other Christian nations moving their embassies to Jerusalem including America, Guatemala, and Honduras.

EZEKIEL 22:29-30

29 The people of the land have used oppressions, committed robbery, and mistreated the poor and needy; and they wrongfully oppress the stranger.

30 So I sought for a man among them who would make a wall, and STAND IN THE GAP before Me on behalf of the land, that I should not destroy it; but I found no one.

A good mediator can make all the difference in the matter of reconciliations. Many enemies just don't have a good mediator. They are too passive, foolish, biased, so needless conflicts prolong in this world.

The greatest unresolved conflict is between God and those who hate Him. So God sent a Mediator to resolve the dispute.

1 TIMOTHY 2:5 (NLT)

For, There is one God and one Mediator who can reconcile God and humanity—the man Christ Jesus.

GALATIANS 3:19 (NLT)

19 ...God gave his law through angels to Moses, who was the mediator between God and the people.

20 Now a mediator is helpful if more than one party must reach an agreement...

HEBREWS 12:24 (NLT)

You have come to Jesus, the one who mediates the new covenant between God and people, and to the sprinkled blood, which speaks of forgiveness instead of crying out for vengeance like the blood of Abel.

If you know that you are distant from God and need a mediator to bring you back into a right relationship with Him before you die, then call on Jesus. At the point of death, it's too late, because all judgments will be recorded against you. You must accept mediation before judgment; this judgment is forever.

The Mediator is Christ Jesus and He qualifies to reconcile you to God because He had no sin and offered to make peace between you and God by dying for all your sins. If you'd like to accept this settlement of all eternal debts and sins, pray this prayer loud enough that you can hear yourself:

"Father God, I'm sorry that my sins have put a distance between me and a Holy God. I accept the Mediator's offer to reconcile my broken relationship with God. I ask You, Father God, to accept my faith in the Blood of Jesus Christ as the complete and final payment for all my sins. Thank You for making me Your child and Heaven my home—when the hour comes for me to depart. I surrender my life to Your Son Jesus and call Him my Lord and Savior now and forever. Amen."

If you have just prayed that prayer in sincerity, congratulations! Your life will never be the same. Not only will God use President Trump, He will use you to fulfill His eternal purpose. Please email team@discoverchurch.online to let us know your decision to follow Jesus.

ACTS 2:38 (NIV)

Peter replied, "Repent and be baptized, every one of you, in the name of Jesus Christ for the forgiveness of your sins. And you will receive the gift of the Holy Spirit."

Your next steps are to be water baptized and to receive the baptism of the Holy Spirit. A good Bible-centered church that believes in the Divinity of Jesus and the present-day work of the Holy Spirit can help you with both. It's important for all Christians to grow in a Bible-centered fellowship. If you are looking for a church locally, our ministry may be able to help you find one. Or if you're looking for an online church, then join one of our Christian communities here: https://discoverchurch.online.

Last but not least, we have one final achievement to highlight in 2020.

September 9, 2020 — President Trump was nominated for the Nobel Peace Prize for his work in brokering the peace agreement between Israel and the United Arab Emirates (UAE).

The nomination was submitted by a four-term member of the Norwegian Parliament, Christian Tybring-Gjedde, who lauded Trump for his key role in establishing normal relations between the two countries. In his nomination letter, he wrote:

"As it is expected other Middle Eastern countries will follow in the footsteps of the UAE, this agreement could be a game changer that will turn the Middle East into a region of cooperation and prosperity."[49]

Tybring-Gjedde said in a Fox News interview: "For his merit, I think he has done more trying to create peace between nations than most other Peace Prize nominees."[50]

Two days later, Bahrain announced it would follow the UAE and normalize relations with Israel.[51] And Trump was nominated for a second time for brokering a peace deal between Serbia and Kosovo.

Magnus Jacobsson, a member of the Swedish Parliament, submitted his nomination letter commending Trump and those two former enemies for their "joint work for peace and economic development, through the cooperation agreement signed in the White House...Trade and communications are important building blocks for peace."[52]

I had predicted this in a video posted on YouTube on June 15, 2018, titled "TRUMP Will Win Nobel PEACE Prize | ART of the DEAL with Kim Jong-Un & Dennis Rodman."[53] A lot of people mocked my prediction two years and two months ago.

Donald Trump deserved it for negotiating with North Korea, halting nuclear tests by the regime, and getting hostages returned home without paying the dictatorship a single dime. He deserved it for negotiating the Israel-UAE peace agreement. He deserved it for negotiating economic normalization between Serbia and Kosovo. But most of all, he deserved it for being the first President in our lifetime not to start a new war during his first term in office. Whether the Norwegian committee will give the prize to him or not, his more prestigious reward is with our Lord in Heaven.

1 KINGS 5:12

So the Lord gave Solomon wisdom, as He had promised him; and there was PEACE between Hiram and Solomon, and the two of them made a treaty together.

PROVERBS 29:14 (ISV)

When a king faithfully administers JUSTICE to the poor, his throne will be established forever.

CHAPTER 8

WHAT'S NEXT?

If anyone without the name Trump had accomplished all these things listed in this book, every Christian would shout for joy. Donald Trump has accomplished so much that is good for Christians. He has unashamedly stood for issues we deeply care about.

Yet you wouldn't know it if you believed only the controlled media. After researching for this book for my readers, I've come to the conclusion that:

- If you were held hostage by terrorists, you would have no better friend than President Trump and his Administration, men like Mike Pence and Mike Pompeo, who are guided by their Christian convictions that religious liberty and freedom from oppression are God-given human rights.

- If you are a persecuted Christian, you would have no better friend than President Trump and his Administration, who were willing to collapse the Turkish economy to free one Christian pastor held in jail. I know of no other world leader with the will or the power to do so. Previous US Presidents left Christians to suffer in Iran and North Korea. Christians were not a priority but a pawn in their geopolitical game.

- If you are a black man or woman unjustly incarcerated for a long time for non-violent crimes, you would have no better friend than President Trump and his Administration. Kim Kardashian—no fan of Trump—was able to meet with him in the Oval Office and plead for clemency on behalf of Alice Marie Johnson, which he granted.

Four more years of this leadership will change the world. Many more Christians will rise to positions of influence. God has an agenda for America, and if America is safe and secure, tyrants will be uncomfortable, globalists will be held in check, and We the People can breathe the air of freedom. America is important in God's plan.

So what is next?

Donald Trump has unfinished business. This is the only reason he will be re-elected. It's time to "Make America GODLY Again."

Trump's second term will be an opportunity for him to implement God's own 10 agendas based on the 10 Commandments. God's standards of justice apply to our modern world and it's not as difficult as you may think, but it does require prayer and creative thinking. I outlined the 10 things that will turn America around in *Trump's Unfinished Business: 10 Prophecies to Save America.*

But there is a hurdle, and it's a big one.

Historically, US Presidents have done worse in their second term than in their first. Their second term is when they make their biggest mistakes. Richard Nixon won his second term by a landslide with 60% of the popular vote in 1972, yet he demolished his legacy by the Watergate scandal and had to resign by August 9, 1974.

Barack Obama won his second term in 2012 and immediately started making his worst blunders: he told the biggest lie of 2013 to sell Obamacare to the American people[1]; he allowed ISIS to rise in 2014—terror, church attacks and decapitations spread wild globally; he negotiated the worst deal perhaps in US history in 2015—the Iran Nuclear Deal, empowering America's enemy.

Woodrow Wilson expanded government overreach in his second term and did serious harm to the US Constitution. Re-elected in 1916, he asked Congress to declare war on Germany in 1917, signed into law the Espionage Act in 1917 and the Sedition Act in 1918. Legal minds have called these acts a declaration of war on the First Amendment itself.[2]

Under these new laws, the US government persecuted and jailed Americans for expressing dissent and pacifism. One pacifist Eugene Debs was arrested, tried and sentenced to 10 years in prison under the Sedition Act after delivering an anti-war speech in June 1918.[3] The erosion of freedom of speech, guaranteed by the First Amendment, really began in Wilson's second term.

Thus the success of winning a second term has often had deleterious effects on Presidents and on the country. The only check that truly holds a powerful man is himself, or better put, his decision to submit himself under God's rule.

1 PETER 5:5-6

5 ...God resists the proud, But gives grace to the humble.

6 Therefore humble yourselves under the mighty hand of God, that He may exalt you in due time,

It will be a challenge for President Trump to be more

humble, more prayerful, and more devoted to Jesus Christ during his second term. The Ten Commandments have been given as his guide to govern, not his guide to Heaven. We are not saved from our personal sins by trying to keep the Ten Commandments; we are saved by grace through faith in Jesus as the only sinless Savior.

But national salvation depends on just leaders, just policies, and a just government. A nation cannot have justice without the Ten Commandments. They are God's principles for Christian leaders to apply to the toughest challenges the world will ever face, including climate change, digital privacy and online rights, gender equality, judicial accountability, family law, and education reform. All the solutions are already there.

DEUTERONOMY 30:11, 14-15 (NIV)

11 Now what I am commanding you today is not too difficult for you or beyond your reach.

14 No, the word is very near you; it is in your mouth and in your heart so you may obey it.

15 See, I set before you today life and prosperity, death and destruction.

CLAIM YOUR REWARD

Congratulations, you've come to the end of the book! Would you like a cheat sheet version of this book that condenses the Presidential highlights into one quick reference?

It's FREE as a token of appreciation for your honest and courteous review on Amazon or Goodreads. Please screenshot your book review[1] and email it to: info@discover.org.au.

Then you will receive your free PDF with over 120 events listed by dates and also categorized by topics. Keep it, refer to it, and you can help us add to it, too. We'd love to hear from you!

Together, let's *Make America GODLY Again!*

Here are the quick links:
Amazon: http://amazon.com/author/newyorktimesbestseller
Goodreads: https://www.goodreads.com/author/show/2119605.Steve_Cioccolanti

NOTES

Introduction

1. Only the most partisan Trump-haters would accuse Trump of laziness, as Bill Clinton did at the DNC2020, when he contrasted Joe Biden as a "man of action," implying Trump was not.
2. https://www.judiciary.senate.gov/imo/media/doc/Epstein%20Testimony.pdf
3. https://www.nytimes.com/2020/08/25/us/politics/trump-hostages.html
4. The Trans-Pacific Partnership (TPP) was a proposed trade agreement between Australia, Brunei, Canada, Chile, Japan, Malaysia, Mexico, New Zealand, Peru, Singapore, Vietnam, and the United States signed by the Obama administration on February 4, 2016.
5. The North American Free Trade Agreement (NAFTA) was a trade agreement between Canada, Mexico, and the United States, proposed by Ronald Reagan, negotiated by George H. W. Bush in 1992, and signed by Bill Clinton in 1993. It was in effect from in 1994-2020. Donald Trump replaced it with the United States—Mexico—Canada Agreement (USMCA), which came into effect on July 1, 2020.
6. https://www.nytimes.com/2020/06/02/world/europe/trump-merkel-allies.html

Statement of Purpose

1. Follow my twitter account at http://www.Twitter.com/cioccolanti
2. https://www.bloomberg.com/politics/articles/2016-07-19/trump-is-richer-in-property-and-deeper-in-debt-in-new-valuation
3. https://www.forbes.com/profile/donald-trump/?list=billionaires#151dc8f647bd

1. Is Trump God's Choice?

1. The infamous line "Read my lips—no new taxes" was a promise made by presidential candidate George H. W. Bush at the Republican National Convention on August 18, 1988.

2. A lie told many times by President Barack Obama in 2013. https://www.politifact.com/article/2013/dec/12/lie-year-if-you-like-your-health-care-plan-keep-it/
3. https://thehill.com/opinion/healthcare/486134-obamacare-10-years-of-distress-and-disappointment
4. https://www.hhs.gov/about/news/2017/05/23/hhs-report-average-health-insurance-premiums-doubled-2013.html
5. Matthew 11:18, Mark 1:6
6. https://www.heritage.org/judicialtracker
7. America has 13 circuit courts or courts of appeal. They are the second most powerful courts in the land, the last stop before the Supreme Court.
8. https://townhall.com/columnists/waynegrudem/2020/08/24/30-good-things-president-trump-has-done-for-america-n2574849
9. https://townhall.com/columnists/waynegrudem/2020/08/24/30-good-things-president-trump-has-done-for-america-n2574849
10. https://www.washingtonpost.com/politics/one-in-every-four-circuit-court-judges-is-now-a-trump-appointee/2019/12/21/d6fa1e98-2336-11ea-bed5-880264cc91a9_story.html
11. https://www.dailywire.com/news/california-state-senator-fights-for-bill-that-could-alter-sex-offender-registration-for-gay-sex-with-minors
12. https://variety.com/2020/film/global/zangro-sundance-cuties-1203467120/
13. https://www.whitehouse.gov/briefings-statements/remarks-president-trump-47th-annual-march-life/
14. https://www.jpost.com/arab-israeli-conflict/lebanons-president-says-country-could-consider-peace-with-israel-638806
15. https://www.aa.com.tr/en/middle-east/beirut-explosion-death-toll-rises-to-171/1938480
16. “Orange man” is a pejorative term Trump’s critics call him. “Orange man bad” is a meme caption that has entered urban slang. It means “a parody expression used to mock critics of President Donald Trump” according to https://knowyourmeme.com/memes/orange-man-bad
17. https://maxlucado.com/decency-for-president/
18. https://www.msnbc.com/rachel-maddow-show/abroad-trump-leaves-us-isolated-ridiculed-pitied-n1223326
19. https://www.theatlantic.com/international/archive/2018/03/trump-xi-jinping-dictators/554810/
20. https://summit.news/2020/08/19/australia-authorities-give-themselves-power-to-remove-children-from-parents-to-ensure-covid-compliance/
21. You can see options to subscribe to our online church community at https://discoverchurch.online. We have Christians and pastors who testify how encouraged they are by being a part. You would be very welcome to join.

22. Recently on July 20, 2020, Texas Republican and former Navy SEAL Rep. Dan Crenshaw proposed a bill that the Space Force dump Air Force rankings and adopt Navy rankings to distinguish it from the Air Force. https://www.airforcemag.com/house-proposal-could-give-naval-ranks-to-space-force/

2. Christian Criticism of Candidate Trump

1. Just before this book with publication, I contacted Max Lucado's ministry to clarify his position. On Sep 4, 2020, I emailed to find out: do you still believe that the President is not a decent man and have your views changed since your blog in 2016? A staff member replied the next day: "Max certainly supports President Trump, as the elected leader of the United States." This is a positive statement, but I still do not know the answer to either question. I must leave it to the reader to decide.
2. https://maxlucado.com/decency-for-president/
3. https://www.faithwire.com/2019/07/08/rugby-australia-says-bible-itself-is-the-problem-in-stunning-admission-about-israel-folaus-firing/
4. https://www.theepochtimes.com/nearly-200-people-arrested-in-australia-for-deliberately-lighting-bushfires_3195827.html
5. https://www.sbs.com.au/news/scott-morrison-blasts-israel-folau-for-appallingly-insensitive-fire-comments
6. https://www.telegraph.co.uk/news/2020/09/01/tony-abbott-rails-against-covid-health-dictatorships-saying/
7. https://quadrant.org.au/opinion/qed/2020/08/australia-how-have-you-let-it-come-to-this/
8. https://www.theguardian.com/australia-news/2020/sep/03/victoria-police-arrested-pregnant-woman-facebook-post-zoe-buhler-australia-warn-lockdown-protesters
9. Isaiah 9:7, 1 Kings 2:45, 1 Kings 9:5, 2 Chronicles 21:7, Isaiah 9:7, Ezekiel 37:25,
10. https://www.christianitytoday.com/ct/1999/november15/47.0.html
11. I pick it because I love the city, I've preached there, and Pastor Max Lucado lives there. It's a serene place with charming riverwalks. I call it the 'Venice of Texas.'
12. Prior to Trump, the Johnson Amendment was interpreted as a gag order preventing pastors from preaching about politics. President Trump vowed that pastors could preach freely without fear of the Johnson Amendment.
13. Jesus said to the religious men who wanted to stone an adulterous woman, "He who is without sin among you, let him throw a stone at her first." (John 8:7)
14. https://www.YouTube.com/DiscoverMinistries

15. https://www.youtube.com/watch?v=WaPb3_ZDO1o
16. Namely, Michael Avenatti and Jussie Smollett.
17. https://www.theguardian.com/us-news/video/2020/may/22/joe-biden-charlamagne-you-aint-black-trump-video

3. Pre-Presidential Timeline: 1946-2016

1. https://en.wikipedia.org/wiki/June_1946_lunar_eclipse
2. https://www.archives.gov/education/lessons/us-israel
3. https://www.timeanddate.com/date/durationresult.html?m1=6&d1=14&y1=1946&m2=5&d2=14&y2=1948
4. https://www.jfklibrary.org/archives/other-resources/john-f-kennedy-speeches/american-newspaper-publishers-association-19610427
5. Sitting presidents assassinated:
    1. Abraham Lincoln (1865)
    2. James A. Garfield (1881)
    3. William McKinley (1901)
    4. John F. Kennedy (1963).
6. https://www.britannica.com/topic/conspiracy
7. https://www.ajc.com/blog/politics/that-time-when-donald-trump-saved-georgia-farm/oYBPGrQx9J33rSDHL5wjcK/
8. https://www.msnbc.com/all-in/watch/donald-trumps-favorite-book-505029187689
9. https://www.presidency.ucsb.edu/documents/press-release-couple-stopped-help-donald-trump-when-his-limo-broke-down-heres-how-he
10. https://www.chron.com/neighborhood/katy/opinion/article/Trump-insisted-on-including-Jews-blacks-at-Palm-9702222.php
11. https://www.nytimes.com/2000/02/19/opinion/what-i-saw-at-the-revolution.html
12. Sitting shiva is the practice of mourning for 7 days after the burial of a loved one.
13. https://www.haaretz.com/world-news/what-do-we-know-about-trumps-pick-as-ambassador-to-israel-1.5459816
14. https://imemc.org/article/trump-donated-10000-to-beit-el-settlement/
15. The O'Reilly Factor was the #1 cable news show for many years during the time it aired from 1996 to 2017.
16. https://www.youtube.com/watch?reload=9&v=bi1fBUgYjAU
17. Ibid.
18. https://en.wikipedia.org/wiki/Dennis_Rodman
19. https://www.washingtonpost.com/news/worldviews/wp/2017/06/15/dennis-rodman-just-gave-kim-jong-un-the-art-of-the-deal-and-it-may-be-a-genius-move/
20. https://vault.si.com/vault/2013/07/08/dennis-rodman

21. When the press wants to discredit someone, even if they sound reasonable or are successful, they tend to use the label "bizarre," as in a "bizarre rant" or "bizarre interview." Here's one example: https://web.archive.org/web/20130304204424/http://www.washingtonpost.com/blogs/the-fix/wp/2013/03/03/dennis-rodman-kim-jong-un-is-my-friend/
22. https://buffalonews.com/news/local/bus-driver-receives-trump-check-headed-for-rachael-ray-show/article_4b3d63d3-ce36-50a2-99f7-aba79d9326d8.html
23. 26 is the number of YHWH or the Name of God in Hebrew. To those who study Bible codes, these numbers when related to an event of spiritual importance are not coincidences. See my books "The DIVINE CODE: A Prophetic Encyclopedia of Numbers, Vol. 1 & 2" on Amazon.
    Volume 1: https://amzn.to/39E9tpe
    Volume 2: https://amzn.to/2QovzdR
24. https://www.politico.com/story/2015/09/donald-trumps-evangelicals-televangelists-214250
25. https://abcnews.go.com/Politics/meet-pastors-support-donald-trump/story?id=38406350
26. https://abcnews.go.com/Politics/meet-pastors-support-donald-trump/story?id=38406350
27. https://www.youtube.com/watch?v=VGoxlByxwoY
28. https://en.wikipedia.org/wiki/United_States_military_casualties_of_war
29. https://www.lohud.com/story/news/local/westchester/2016/06/01/1-million-trump-bump-veterans-charity-tuckahoe/85241126/
30. https://boston.cbslocal.com/2016/05/31/donald-trump-donates-75k-to-new-england-wounded-veterans-charity/
31. Ibid.
32. https://www.npr.org/2016/06/21/483018976/inside-trumps-closed-door-meeting-held-to-reassures-the-evangelicals
33. https://www.npr.org/2016/06/21/483018976/inside-trumps-closed-door-meeting-held-to-reassures-the-evangelicals
34. https://www.facebook.com/watch/?v=10154505452562378&extid=Mql4MmnVRtKyiNvT
35. https://www.abc.net.au/news/2016-09-13/black-pastor-darrell-scott-on-why-he-supports-donald-trump/7836872
36. Ibid.
37. https://www.breitbart.com/politics/2020/08/12/kamala-harris-young-people-are-stupid-they-make-really-bad-decisions/
38. https://grabien.com/story.php?id=232235
39. https://www.nationalreview.com/2019/04/kamala-harris-impeachment-voting-age-changes/
40. https://afropunk.com/2019/01/kamala-harris-has-been-tough-on-black-people-not-crime/

41. https://www.cnn.com/2019/01/18/politics/kamala-harris-criminal-justice/index.html
42. https://www.businessinsider.com/californias-kamala-harris-becomes-first-indian-american-us-senator-2016-11
43. https://www.newsweek.com/kamala-harris-makes-history-first-black-woman-vp-nominee-1521475
44. Charlotta Bass was the first black woman to run for VP on the Progressive Party ticket in 1952.
45. https://www.cnn.com/2019/01/18/politics/kamala-harris-criminal-justice/index.html

4. First Year: 2017

1. https://www.youtube.com/watch?v=cRnmAdkqHog
2. https://www.csmonitor.com/USA/Foreign-Policy/2017/0124/Why-Trump-froze-funding-to-overseas-groups-that-promote-abortion
3. https://www.whitehouse.gov/presidential-actions/presidential-memorandum-regarding-mexico-city-policy/
4. https://www.whitehouse.gov/briefings-statements/president-trump-takes-action-expedite-priority-energy-infrastructure-projects/
5. https://www.rt.com/news/500506-israel-bahrain-relations-trump-us/
6. https://www.whitehouse.gov/presidential-actions/executive-order-enhancing-public-safety-interior-united-states/
7. Press Release, "President Trump's Meeting With Immigration Crime Victims," The Whitehouse, June 29, 2017, https://www.whitehouse.gov/articles/president-trumps-meeting-immigration-crime-victims/
8. https://www.whitehouse.gov/presidential-actions/presidential-executive-order-reducing-regulation-controlling-regulatory-costs/
9. https://www.whitehouse.gov/briefings-statements/president-donald-j-trumps-historic-deregulatory-actions-creating-greater-opportunity-prosperity-americans/
10. https://www.whitehouse.gov/presidential-actions/president-donald-j-trump-nominates-judge-neil-gorsuch-united-states-supreme-court/
11. https://www.nytimes.com/2017/02/07/us/politics/betsy-devos-education-secretary-confirmed.html
12. https://townhall.com/columnists/waynegrudem/2020/08/24/30-good-things-president-trump-has-done-for-america-n2574849
13. https://edition.cnn.com/2017/02/03/politics/f-35-lockheed-martin-cost-reduction/index.html
14. https://www.reuters.com/article/us-usa-trump-lgbt/trump-revokes-obama-guidelines-on-transgender-bathrooms-idUSKBN161243
15. https://www.jacksonlewis.com/sites/default/files/docs/2-22-17%20guidance_letter.pdf

16. https://www.whitehouse.gov/presidential-actions/remarks-president-trump-signing-hbcu-executive-order/
17. https://theundefeated.com/features/trump-signs-executive-order-on-hbcus/
18. https://www.wusa9.com/article/news/local/verify/verify-has-trump-given-more-money-to-hbcus-than-any-other-president/65-543185506
19. 40 is the number of trial. 44 is the number of child.
20. https://twitter.com/realDonaldTrump/status/837989835818287106
    https://twitter.com/realDonaldTrump/status/837996746236182529
21. 58 is the number of Noah and of grace. In Hebrew, 58 literally spells "Noah" and backwards spells "grace." A victory by 58 votes is befitting the gracious, soft-spoke doctor. 58 appears many times in Donald Trump's life. He is the 45th president, but his was the 58th inauguration. See more in my books "The DIVINE CODE: A Prophetic Encyclopedia of Numbers, Vol. 1 & 2"
    Volume 1: https://amzn.to/39E9tpe
    Volume 2: https://amzn.to/2QovzdR
22. https://religionnews.com/2016/02/01/ben-carson-religion-adventist-evangelical/
23. https://abc7.com/first-100-days-president-donald-trump-potus/1924621/
24. https://abc7.com/first-100-days-president-donald-trump-potus/1924621/
25. https://www.whitehouse.gov/presidential-actions/president-donald-j-trump-proclaims-may-2017-jewish-american-heritage-month/
26. https://www.whitehouse.gov/briefings-statements/remarks-president-trump-signing-executive-order-america-first-offshore-energy-strategy/
27. https://abcnews.go.com/Politics/trump-100-days-successful-us-history/story?id=47100880
28. https://www.whitehouse.gov/presidential-actions/presidential-executive-order-promoting-free-speech-religious-liberty/
29. https://www.whitehouse.gov/presidential-actions/president-donald-j-trump-proclaims-may-4-2017-national-day-prayer/
30. Trump, Ibid.
31. https://www.whitehouse.gov/briefings-statements/statement-president-trump-paris-climate-accord/
32. https://www.whitehouse.gov/briefings-statements/statement-president-trump-paris-climate-accord/
33. https://www.whitehouse.gov/articles/president-trump-announces-u-s-withdrawal-paris-climate-accord/
34. https://www.whitehouse.gov/briefings-statements/statement-american-citizens-unjustly-detained-iran/
35. https://www.whitehouse.gov/presidential-actions/presidential-executive-order-imposing-sanctions-respect-situation-venezuela/
36. http://money.visualcapitalist.com/richer-poorer-venezuela-economic-tragedy/

37. Ibid.
38. https://www.usnews.com/news/national-news/articles/2017-08-31/trump-to-donate-1-million-to-harvey-relief-white-house-says
39. https://www.whitehouse.gov/briefings-statements/remarks-president-trump-joint-address-congress/
40. https://www.whitehouse.gov/briefings-statements/president-donald-j-trump-restores-responsibility-rule-law-immigration/
41. https://www.whitehouse.gov/presidential-actions/president-donald-j-trump-proclaims-friday-september-8-2017-sunday-september-10-2017-national-days-prayer-remembrance/
42. https://www.justice.gov/opa/press-release/file/1001891/download?utm_medium=email&utm_source=govdelivery
43. Ibid.
44. https://www.whitehouse.gov/briefings-statements/statement-president-donald-j-trump-recovering-boyle-coleman-family-captivity-pakistan/
45. https://www.christianpost.com/news/trump-admin-motions-to-argue-on-behalf-of-jack-phillips-in-supreme-court-gay-wedding-cake-case.html
46. https://www.nbcnews.com/feature/nbc-out/masterpiece-cakeshop-owner-court-again-denying-lgbtq-customer-n1184656
47. TRUMP'S UNFINISHED BUSINESS: 10 PROPHECIES TO SAVE AMERICA.
    Paperback: https://amzn.to/339yUgc
    Ebook: https://amzn.to/2IC7iXj
48. https://www.whitehouse.gov/presidential-actions/president-donald-j-trump-proclaims-november-9-2017-world-freedom-day/
49. https://www.whitehouse.gov/presidential-actions/president-donald-j-trump-proclaims-november-19-november-25-2017-national-family-week/
50. 22 is the number of the Jews, the number of letters in the Jewish alphabet, the number of years Jacob and Joseph suffered. It is no surprise that many 22's appear in Trump's administration. See its end time meaning in my books "The DIVINE CODE: A Prophetic Encyclopedia of Numbers, Vol. 1 & 2"
    Volume 1: https://amzn.to/39E9tpe
    Volume 2: https://amzn.to/2QovzdR
51. https://www.whitehouse.gov/presidential-actions/presidential-proclamation-recognizing-jerusalem-capital-state-israel-relocating-united-states-embassy-israel-jerusalem/
52. https://www.whitehouse.gov/presidential-actions/president-donald-j-trump-proclaims-december-10-2017-human-rights-day-december-15-2017-bill-rights-day-week-beginning-december-10-2017-human-rights-week/
53. https://www.whitehouse.gov/briefings-statements/president-trump-commutes-sentence-sholom-rubashkin/

54. https://www.whitehouse.gov/briefings-statements/tax-cuts-act-follows-president-donald-j-trumps-promise-middle-class-tax-cuts/
55. The Organisation of Economic Co-operation and Development (OECD) average corporate tax is 22.5 percent.
56. https://www.washingtontimes.com/news/2015/apr/27/obama-backed-green-energy-failures-leave-taxpayers/
57. https://www.thedailybeast.com/cheats/2014/09/24/obamacare-websites-cost-over-2b
58. https://www.whitehouse.gov/presidential-actions/executive-order-blocking-property-persons-involved-serious-human-rights-abuse-corruption/
59. https://www.whitehouse.gov/presidential-actions/president-donald-j-trump-proclaims-january-2018-national-slavery-human-trafficking-prevention-month/

5. Second Year: 2018

1. https://www.whitehouse.gov/presidential-actions/president-donald-j-trump-proclaims-january-16-2018-religious-freedom-day/
2. https://www.whitehouse.gov/presidential-actions/president-donald-j-trump-proclaims-january-22-2018-national-sanctity-human-life-day/
3. https://www.weforum.org/agenda/2018/01/president-donald-trumps-davos-address-in-full-8e14ebc1-79bb-4134-8203-95efca182e94/
4. https://www.weforum.org/agenda/2018/01/president-donald-trumps-davos-address-in-full-8e14ebc1-79bb-4134-8203-95efca182e94/
5. https://www.whitehouse.gov/presidential-actions/presidential-proclamation-death-billy-graham/
6. https://www.frcaction.org/accomplishments
7. https://www.whitehouse.gov/presidential-actions/president-donald-j-trump-proclaims-april-2018-national-child-abuse-prevention-month/
8. https://www.whitehouse.gov/presidential-actions/president-donald-j-trump-proclaims-april-12-april-19-2018-days-remembrance-victims-holocaust/
9. https://web.archive.org/web/20200411102902/https://www.state.gov/being-a-christian-leader/
10. https://www.whitehouse.gov/briefings-statements/remarks-president-trump-president-buhari-federal-republic-nigeria-bilateral-meeting/
11. https://www.whitehouse.gov/presidential-actions/president-donald-j-trump-proclaims-may-3-national-day-prayer/
12. https://www.usatoday.com/story/opinion/2018/05/08/iran-nuclear-deal-worst-donald-trump-column/589828002/

13. https://www.whitehouse.gov/presidential-actions/ceasing-u-s-participation-jcpoa-taking-additional-action-counter-irans-malign-influence-deny-iran-paths-nuclear-weapon/
14. Hazmat is an abbreviation for hazardous materials.
15. https://wallbuilders.com/americas-biblically-hostile-u-s-president/
16. https://abc7news.com/north-korea-detainees-north-korea-kim-jong-un-donald-trump/3449859/
17. https://www.whitehouse.gov/briefings-statements/statement-vice-president-mike-pence-release-three-americans/
18. https://www.whitehouse.gov/briefings-statements/wtas-trump-administration-secures-release-three-americans-north-korea/
19. https://www.whitehouse.gov/briefings-statements/wtas-trump-administration-secures-release-three-americans-north-korea/
20. https://www.whitehouse.gov/briefings-statements/statement-press-secretary-regarding-pardon-john-arthur-jack-johnson/
21. 1 Corinthians 15:42, 50; Romans 8:21; Luke 20:35; Daniel 12:3.
22. https://www.whitehouse.gov/presidential-actions/president-donald-j-trump-proclaims-memorial-day-may-28-2018-day-prayer-permanent-peace/
23. https://www.deseret.com/utah/2020/8/5/21354632/hope-in-darkness-2-year-nightmare-ends-josh-holt-and-wife-gain-freedom
24. https://en.wikipedia.org/wiki/Dinesh_D%27Souza
25. https://www.whitehouse.gov/briefings-statements/statement-press-secretary-regarding-pardon-dinesh-dsouza/
26. https://web.archive.org/web/20100827014331/http://www.christianitytoday.com/ct/2010/augustweb-only/44-21.0.html
27. https://www.whitehouse.gov/briefings-statements/president-trump-commutes-sentence-alice-marie-johnson/
28. https://www.whitehouse.gov/briefings-statements/remarks-president-trump-granting-full-pardon-alice-johnson/
29. https://www.whitehouse.gov/presidential-actions/president-donald-j-trump-announces-intent-nominate-judge-brett-m-kavanaugh-supreme-court-united-states/
30. https://www.whitehouse.gov/briefings-statements/remarks-vice-president-pence-ministerial-advance-religious-freedom/
31. https://www.youtube.com/watch?v=aYsaC2CADs0
32. https://en.wikipedia.org/wiki/2018_North_Korea–United_States_Singapore_Summit
33. https://www.cnbc.com/2019/02/15/trump-obama-told-me-that-he-was-close-to-starting-a-big-war-with-north-korea.html
34. https://www.whitehouse.gov/briefings-statements/president-trump-commutes-sentence-ted-suhl/
35. https://www.reuters.com/article/us-turkey-currency-erdogan-idUSKBN1KW08U

36. https://www.whitehouse.gov/briefings-statements/remarks-president-trump-meeting-inner-city-pastors/
37. https://www.youtube.com/watch?v=nW8sC9JA2Is
38. The Johnson amendment (1954) forbade churches from putting out their political preferences under threat of losing their tax exemptions. It also meant that anyone who donated to them couldn't claim that donation as a tax-deductible gift. The law has not been changed yet, but President Trump issued an executive order that limits the Treasury from enforcing it strictly.
39. https://www.whitehouse.gov/briefings-statements/remarks-president-trump-dinner-evangelical-leaders/
40. https://www.whitehouse.gov/presidential-actions/presidential-proclamation-national-days-prayer-remembrance-2018/
41. https://www.whitehouse.gov/presidential-actions/presidential-proclamation-national-gang-violence-prevention-week-2018/
42. https://www.washingtonexaminer.com/washington-secrets/trumps-list-289-accomplishments-in-just-20-months-relentless-promise-keeping
43. https://www.whitehouse.gov/briefings-statements/remarks-president-trump-meeting-pastor-andrew-brunson/
44. https://thehill.com/policy/healthcare/247850-court-rules-nuns-group-must-comply-with-obamacare-birth-control-mandate
45. https://en.wikipedia.org/wiki/Burwell_v._Hobby_Lobby_Stores,_Inc.
46. https://www.frcaction.org/accomplishments
47. https://en.wikipedia.org/wiki/Speedy_Trial_Clause
48. https://www.foxnews.com/politics/trump-signs-executive-order-giving-christmas-eve-off-to-federal-employees
49. https://jeffries.house.gov/2018/12/21/collins-jeffries-historic-criminal-justice-reform-bill-signed-into-law/

6. Third Year: 2019

1. https://www.congress.gov/bill/115th-congress/house-bill/2200
2. https://www.congress.gov/bill/115th-congress/senate-bill/1862
3. https://www.congress.gov/bill/115th-congress/house-bill/672
4. https://www.whitehouse.gov/presidential-actions/presidential-proclamation-religious-freedom-day-2019/
5. https://www.whitehouse.gov/presidential-actions/presidential-proclamation-national-sanctity-human-life-day-2019/
6. https://www.whitehouse.gov/briefings-statements/remarks-president-trump-2019-national-prayer-breakfast/
7. https://townhall.com/columnists/waynegrudem/2020/08/24/30-good-things-president-trump-has-done-for-america-n2574849

8. https://www.nbcnews.com/politics/donald-trump/trump-begins-one-one-kim-jong-un-tempering-expectations-n977466
9. https://www.foxnews.com/politics/trump-on-cpac-stage-with-berkeley-assault-victim-promises-executive-order-on-campus-free-speech
10. https://www.foxnews.com/politics/trump-signs-executive-order-to-promote-free-speech-on-college-campuses
11. https://www.whitehouse.gov/briefings-statements/president-donald-j-trump-is-improving-transparency-and-promoting-free-speech-in-higher-education/
12. https://www.whitehouse.gov/briefings-statements/wall-street-journal-trump-issue-order-tying-federal-grants-free-speech-campus/
13. https://www.whitehouse.gov/presidential-actions/proclamation-recognizing-golan-heights-part-state-israel/
14. https://www.whitehouse.gov/briefings-statements/remarks-president-trump-2019-prison-reform-summit-first-step-act-celebration/
15. https://townhall.com/columnists/waynegrudem/2020/08/24/30-good-things-president-trump-has-done-for-america-n2574849
16. https://www.whitehouse.gov/briefings-statements/remarks-president-trump-national-day-prayer-service/
17. https://www.whitehouse.gov/presidential-actions/proclamation-prayer-peace-memorial-day-2019/
18. https://www.whitehouse.gov/briefings-statements/president-donald-j-trump-tearing-red-tape-order-build-affordable-housing/
19. https://www.nbcnews.com/politics/donald-trump/trump-kim-jong-un-meet-dmz-n1025041
20. You can get this one-hour teaching on DVD https://discover.org.au/book-shop/topic/pure-desires-psychology-of-love-dvd or stream it now on Vimeo https://vimeo.com/ondemand/puredesireslove
21. https://edition.cnn.com/2018/05/21/us/mike-pompeo-fast-facts/index.html
22. https://edition.cnn.com/2019/07/08/politics/pompeo-unalienable-rights-commission/index.html
23. https://www.state.gov/2019-ministerial-to-advance-religious-freedom/
24. https://www.whitehouse.gov/briefings-statements/remarks-vice-president-pence-2nd-annual-religious-freedom-ministerial/
25. https://www.christianpost.com/news/trump-meets-27-survivors-of-persecution-in-oval-office-learns-about-their-plight.html
26. https://www.jpost.com/international/trump-releases-israeli-drug-smuggler-on-childrens-moving-request-597149
27. https://www.whitehouse.gov/briefings-statements/president-trump-commutes-sentence-ronen-nahmani/
28. https://www.whitehouse.gov/presidential-actions/presidential-proclamation-national-days-prayer-remembrance-2019/
29. https://www.whitehouse.gov/briefings-statements/remarks-president-trump-united-nations-event-religious-freedom-new-york-ny/

30. https://www.whitehouse.gov/presidential-actions/presidential-memorandum-determination-respect-efforts-foreign-governments-regarding-trafficking-persons/
31. https://www.whitehouse.gov/presidential-actions/presidential-proclamation-world-freedom-day-2019/
32. See 1 Kings 12, 2 Chronicles 10.
33. TRUMP'S UNFINISHED BUSINESS: 10 PROPHECIES TO SAVE AMERICA
    Paperback: https://amzn.to/339yUgc
    Ebook: https://amzn.to/2IC7iXj
34. https://www.whitehouse.gov/briefings-statements/statement-press-secretary-regarding-release-two-hostages-taliban/
35. https://www.whitehouse.gov/presidential-actions/presidential-proclamation-human-rights-day-bill-rights-day-human-rights-week-2019/
36. https://apnews.com/c4834e48841d97c5a93312b1bf75302a
37. Ibid.
38. https://www.whitehouse.gov/presidential-actions/proclamation-national-slavery-human-trafficking-prevention-month-2020/

7. Fourth Year: 2020

1. https://www.whitehouse.gov/briefings-statements/remarks-president-trump-killing-qasem-soleimani/
2. https://www.whitehouse.gov/presidential-actions/proclamation-religious-freedom-day-2020/
3. https://www.whitehouse.gov/presidential-actions/proclamation-national-sanctity-human-life-day-2020/
4.
5. https://www.smh.com.au/business/markets/trump-s-speech-at-davos-is-putting-chill-down-european-spines-20200120-p53sym.html
6. https://edition.cnn.com/2020/01/21/business/greta-thunberg-davos/
7. https://www.whitehouse.gov/briefings-statements/remarks-president-trump-world-economic-forum-davos-switzerland/
8. Trump, Ibid.
9. https://www.whitehouse.gov/briefings-statements/remarks-president-trump-47th-annual-march-life/
10. https://www.whitehouse.gov/briefings-statements/president-donald-j-trumps-united-states-mexico-canada-agreement-delivers-historic-win-american-workers/
11. https://www.donaldjtrump.com/media/timeline-the-trump-administrations-decisive-actions-to-combat-the-coronavirus/

12. https://www.wsj.com/articles/the-failed-experiment-of-covid-lockdowns-11599000890
13. No travel to Iran; no entry into the US by foreign nationals who visited Iran in the last 14 days.
14. 22 is the number of end times and the number of chapters in the Book of Revelation. See my books "The DIVINE CODE: A Prophetic Encyclopedia of Numbers, Vol. 1 & 2" available at http://amazon.com/author/newyorktimesbestseller
15. https://www.rt.com/news/485825-trump-halts-who-funding-covid-19/
16. https://hongkongfp.com/2020/04/16/hong-kong-broadcaster-rejects-who-claim-that-interview-with-top-doctor-was-distorted/
17. https://en.wikipedia.org/wiki/Timeline_of_computer_viruses_and_worms
18. https://en.wikipedia.org/wiki/Bill_%26_Melinda_Gates_Foundation
19. As former Prime Minister of Australia Tony Abbott called it: https://www.telegraph.co.uk/news/2020/09/01/tony-abbott-rails-against-covid-health-dictatorships-saying/
20. https://www.nbcnews.com/politics/2020-election/coronavirus-has-ignited-battle-over-voting-my-mail-here-s-n1178531 and https://www.bizpacreview.com/2020/09/03/ag-barr-isnt-having-cheap-talk-sets-wolf-blitzer-straight-on-reckless-and-dangerous-mass-mail-in-voting-967556
21. https://campaignbrief.com/victorian-government-launches-staying-apart-keeps-us-together-campaign-via-mc-saatchi/
22. https://www.whitehouse.gov/briefings-statements/president-trump-leading-generation-effort-ensure-americans-access-covid-19-vaccine/
23. https://www.sciencemag.org/news/2020/05/unveiling-warp-speed-white-house-s-america-first-push-coronavirus-vaccine
24. https://www.whitehouse.gov/briefings-statements/remarks-president-trump-announcing-executive-order-preventing-online-censorship/
25. https://www.jfklibrary.org/archives/other-resources/john-f-kennedy-speeches/american-newspaper-publishers-association-19610427
26. https://www.bakersfield.com/news/two-bakersfield-doctors-cite-their-testing-data-to-urge-reopening/article_eb1959e0-84fa-11ea-9a07-2f2bea880bf9.html
27. For those who want to bypass Big Tech, there are uncensored platforms like Bitchute, an alternative to YouTube.

    The first video of Bakersfield doctors is at: https://tinyurl.com/yd2ey9z4.

    The second video of doctors addressing misinformation is at: https://tinyurl.com/y4d952js.
28. TRUMP'S UNFINISHED BUSINESS: 10 PROPHECIES TO SAVE AMERICA is available as:

    Paperback https://amzn.to/339yUgc

    and E-book: https://amzn.to/2IC7iXj

29. https://www.whitehouse.gov/presidential-actions/executive-order-advancing-international-religious-freedom/
30. A setback for normal social and political events came after Herman Cain, a prominent black conservative, attended the Tulsa Rally without a mask. Nine days later he was diagnosed with COVID19. It is not clear that he contracted it at the rally, but his death on July 30, 2020 was mocked by much of the pro-lockdown media. The truth is that Taiwan has handled both H1N1 and COVID19 epidemics successfully without a lockdown of the economy. Different solutions are possible and need to be studied by the decision makers.
31. https://www.jfklibrary.org/archives/other-resources/john-f-kennedy-speeches/american-newspaper-publishers-association-19610427
32. https://www.rev.com/blog/transcripts/donald-trump-tulsa-oklahoma-rally-speech-transcript
33. https://www.whitehouse.gov/presidential-actions/executive-order-protecting-american-monuments-memorials-statues-combating-recent-criminal-violence/
34. https://www.whitehouse.gov/briefings-statements/president-donald-j-trumps-united-states-mexico-canada-agreement-delivers-historic-win-american-workers/
35. https://www.hhs.gov/about/news/2020/07/08/secretary-azar-statement-on-little-sisters-of-the-poor-supreme-court-ruling.html
36. https://www.whitehouse.gov/articles/congress-didnt-act-on-prescription-drug-prices-so-president-trump-did/
37. https://www.whitehouse.gov/briefings-statements/remarks-vice-president-pence-importance-life-seminole-fl/
38. https://www.whitehouse.gov/articles/president-trump-we-have-rejected-globalism-and-embraced-patriotism/
39. https://www.whitehouse.gov/articles/president-trump-we-have-rejected-globalism-and-embraced-patriotism/
40. In an interview with Jeffrey Goldberg of The Atlantic, Obama said, "I want a president who has the sense that you can't fix everything." https://www.theatlantic.com/magazine/archive/2016/04/the-obama-doctrine/471525/
41. https://www.nbcnews.com/politics/2020-election/rnc-2020-trump-appears-hostages-he-helped-bring-home-u-n1237960
42. Ibid.
43. https://www.newyorker.com/news/news-desk/how-trump-has-reversed-decades-of-american-hostage-policy
44. https://abcnews.go.com/Politics/video/herschel-walker-speaks-2020-rnc-72578797
45. https://www.rev.com/blog/transcripts/jack-brewer-2020-rnc-speech-transcript

46. https://www.abc.net.au/news/2020-08-28/republican-convention-day-four-live-updates/12589344
47. https://edition.cnn.com/2020/08/28/politics/donald-trump-speech-transcript/index.html
48. https://www.whitehouse.gov/briefings-statements/statement-president-regarding-economic-normalization-serbia-kosovo/
49. https://www.foxnews.com/politics/trump-nominated-for-nobel-peace-prize-by-norwegian-official
50. Ibid.
51. https://www.rt.com/news/500506-israel-bahrain-relations-trump-us/
52. https://nypost.com/2020/09/11/donald-trump-nominated-for-second-nobel-peace-prize/?utm_source=facebook_sitebuttons&utm_medium=site+buttons&utm_campaign=site+buttons&fbclid=IwAR3-wcNIRD-szX_qgqQwHPNdQAY5eqUmlOwL77_5QF-PseUpxgbHOKLTT6A
53. https://youtu.be/m_Exvcz6hoY.

    Join 300,000 subscribers at my YouTube channel: https://www.YouTube.com/DiscoverMinistries

8. What's Next?

1. A lie told many times by President Barack Obama in 2013. https://www.politifact.com/article/2013/dec/12/lie-year-if-you-like-your-health-care-plan-keep-it/
2. https://reason.com/2017/09/26/when-the-government-declared-w/
3. https://www.history.com/this-day-in-history/u-s-congress-passes-sedition-act

Claim Your Reward

1. This reward is subject to each book review being fair-minded and tasteful. Insults and anti-religious discrimination will not be rewarded and may be reported to appropriate authorities.

ACKNOWLEDGEMENT

Jesus had a team of twelve. I had seven.
My special thanks to friends and ministry supporters who contributed helpful comments and corrections:

Jacky Choi
Oana Dickinson
Rich Marsh
Marla Nistico
Colette Rhodes
Lorilyn Roberts
Andy Steffen

"God has given each of you a gift from his great variety of spiritual gifts. Use them well to serve one another."
1 Peter 4:10 (NLT)

ABOUT THE AUTHOR

A Christian pastor, author and prolific teacher of God's Word, Steve Cioccolanti has over 300,000 subscribers on social media and more than 45 million views on YouTube. He is a four-time #1 bestselling author on Amazon. Known for his bold prophecies, he predicted Donald Trump's 2016 election victory before he was the Republican Presidential nominee—at that time pundits and pollsters were certain Trump had less than 1% chance of winning.

His books *The Divine Code: A Prophetic Encyclopedia of Numbers, Vol. 1 & 2* revealed many prophetic codes associated with Trump and current global events. The two volumes became instant bestsellers on Amazon.

In February 2020, *Trump's Unfinished Business: 10 Prophecies to Save America* offered Christians and world leaders a reinterpretation of God's 10 Commandments, presented as God's template of justice to "Make America Godly Again."

In his latest book, *President Trump's Pro-Christian Accomplishments*, he lays out the evidence the mainstream media does not want you to see. Donald Trump is not the man they claim him to be. Based on his four-year track record, he may be the most pro-Christian, pro-Church, and pro-Israel President in our lifetime. 2020 has been a year of pandemic and great trial, but God is setting America up for victory. He wants His people live in optimism and rejoice. As Proverbs 29:2 says, "When the righteous are in authority, the people rejoice."

Follow Pastor Cioccolanti's main channel here: www.YouTube.com/DiscoverMinistries.

Stream his high quality videos here: www.vimeo.com/steve-cioccolanti/vod_pages.

Stream the best videos about the Bible and Trump here: https://discoverchurch.online/movies

He is the senior pastor of Discover Church in Melbourne, Australia, and a pioneer of online church, leading a Christian network through a private social media app. Join his online community at: www.discoverchurch.online

To invite Pastor Cioccolanti to your speaking event, check his availability at: www.discover.org.au/invite

Follow his social media updates

ALSO BY STEVE CIOCCOLANTI

🇺🇸 TRUMP'S UNFINISHED BUSINESS:

10 PROPHECIES TO SAVE AMERICA

http://amazon.com/author/newyorktimesbestseller

MOVIES

By Steve Cioccolanti

WATCH ONLINE!

discoverchurch.online/movies

Made in the USA
Columbia, SC
22 November 2021